So Much For Life

Mark Hyatt

Edited by
Sam Ladkin
& Luke Roberts

Nightboat Books
New York

So Much For Life

Selected Poems

Mark Hyatt

Contents

So Much For Life

INTRODUCTION

Mark Hyatt's poetry hurts. This is the central fact the whole way through: his experiences are shattering and his words fall apart in front of him. Moments of softness and tenderness are too fragile to hold onto. His desire is restless and overwhelming. An exhilarating, even self-lacerating energy can turn on a line break into world-weariness and exhaustion. So much for life, writes Hyatt, in a shrug of disappointment addressed to the world at large, his friends, his would-be or ex-lovers, his estranged family and himself. Only somehow, again and again, it all comes together in moments so beautiful and so self-exposed we don't know where to look. So much *for* life, for a frantic commitment to liberation, unapologetically hedonistic, daring, and courageous.

Hyatt died by suicide in April 1972, overdosing on sleeping pills and aspirin in a cave in rural Lancashire. It's hard, knowing this, to avoid the familiar script of the doomed poet, especially when viewing his life in outline: working class and queer in the decades before gay liberation; Romani; a small-time thief and sometime sex worker; incarcerated more than once; subject to electroconvulsive therapy; an intravenous drug user; illiterate until adulthood. Faced with layers of structural oppression and social stigma, Hyatt's poetry resounds with loneliness and desolation. And yet his writing and his life also tell a story of struggle and survival and love. The most shocking thing about these poems is how fresh they feel, calling out to us to see if we're ready.

Hyatt had no writing career to speak of. In the years following his death, his poems would appear in three chapbooks, in little magazines, and the occasional anthology. A handful of dedicated readers kept his poetry in circulation, leaving enough traces to ensure a marginal visibility. He left behind some 1700 pages or more of work, including hundreds of poems, drafts of plays, even a complete novel. Most of the originals were destroyed in a flood, leaving only a xeroxed archive preserved by an act of care and foresight. This is his first full-length book. Alongside the previously unpublished novel *Love, Leda*, it is the first publication to bear his name in almost 50 years.

★

If you love a writer who hardly anyone has heard of and few have read, it's tempting to make grand claims. It's also tempting for us to set down everything we know, every scrap of detail we've managed to glean about Hyatt's short and difficult life. We know, for instance, that Hyatt was a beautiful and terrific dancer. We think James Baldwin took a shine to him at a book party in London in the early 1960s. We know he went to prison in the spring of 1966, and that he claimed it was for 'picking flowers', which sounds like a drugs charge, or what the Wolfenden Report into Homosexual Offences and Prostitution (1957) would call 'importuning'. We know he had conflicted and fraught feelings about religion and was possibly baptised while in hospital in 1971 by a man we know only as 'Cornelius'. So much, however, remains mysterious, and we want to leave Hyatt's reception to his new readers, offering here only a brief sketch of his life, in order to give a sense of the pressures and possibilities of the period.

Details of his early life are hard to come by. He was born on December 20th 1940 in Tooting, on the outskirts of South London. He grew up in poverty. His father, James Hyatt, sold groceries from a horse-drawn cart, worked in a scrapyard, and is listed in the 1939 census as a 'hawker', a street-seller. His mother, Rachel Hilden, was Romani, and died aged 28, when Hyatt was just five years old. His father remarried soon after. As he writes in 'Hashish on Sunday':

> By birth I am a diddikai, my interest
> in rubbish comes from my father's side
> and my flare of mad quick colour from

an unknown mother, unknown to me that is,
if need be I know how to lie, I was fed
with lies from babyhood to teenager
but somewhere after leaving home, I
learned my own kind of truth.

The term 'diddikai', referring to someone of mixed Traveller ancestry, is echoed elsewhere in Hyatt's use of 'half-romani' and 'half-gypsy' as self-identifications. It can carry a pejorative sense and, characteristically for Hyatt, moments of pride quickly mingle with socially inscribed shame and secrecy.

He received little or no formal education, working alongside his father in the market from an early age. Perhaps it's here that he picked up his verbal inventiveness and love of jokes and puns, but his childhood was fundamentally unhappy. References to his father in his writing are uniformly negative, often accompanied by memories of violence: a pivotal scene in *Love, Leda* involves visiting the family home and being brutally attacked for bringing the name into disrepute. As he writes in one of his most extraordinary poems, 'True Homosexual Love': 'Even as a man I still move under the shadow / of a woman's belt or a father's wooded plank.'

We don't know exactly how Hyatt's escape from the social conservatism of his upbringing unfolded, but the grocery cart took him to Covent Garden in central London, close to the coffee houses and hangouts of Soho, crucial to queer life and new youth subcultures. It was there, in a gay club in 1960, that Hyatt met the writer Cressida Lindsay. Soon after, he moved with her to the bohemian enclaves of Notting Hill, staying at a large and dilapidated mansion block, 24 Chepstow Villas.

It was a volatile era. Notting Hill was one of the few places in the city where housing was available to people of colour, offered on exploitative terms by slum landlords with links to organised crime. Fascists openly rallied in the area and 1958 saw a wave of violent attacks on the Black community, including several nights of full-scale rioting. Lindsay – who had been a member of the Communist Party, was unmarried, and had a child with a West Indian musician – wrote about these events in her novels *No Wonderland* (1962) and *Fathers & Lovers* (1969).

The crowd at Chepstow Villas featured a revolving cast of actors, artists, and writers. These included Dudley Sutton, star of the homoerotic motorbike film *The Leather Boys* (1964); the novelist Laura Del-Rivo, author of *The Furnished Room* (1961), which was itself filmed as *West 11* (1963); and Del-Rivo's sister, Lucy O'Shea, who became one of Hyatt's best friends. Hyatt makes small cameos in the novels of his milieu, appearing as Jason – a singer – in *Fathers & Lovers*, and as Jack in Del-Rivo's *Daffodil on the Pavement* (1967). In the latter, his entrance is a breath of fresh air: scandalous, irreverent, playful, he undercuts the jostling egos and intellectual posturing of the angry young men around him.

Hyatt and Lindsay had a child together, Dylan, and their relationship lasted on-and-off until the mid-1960s. Their domestic situation was complicated. Hyatt had a number of boyfriends, including the publisher Anthony Blond – who would later become Lindsay's partner – but his emotional life seems to have been dominated for years by the idealised figure of his neighbour, John Lindsay (no relation), a devout Christian who lived with his wife and children a few doors down.

It was in this environment of cultural stimulation and dramatic social change that Cressida Lindsay taught Hyatt to read and write, an education that continued throughout the decade with the help of various friends and lovers. Writing quickly became the central activity of Hyatt's life, and the poems that have survived are a testament to the frustrations and possibilities of articulation and expression. The status of Hyatt's literacy and process of his composition has been the source of speculation and confusion, as we outline in our editorial notes. His preference was to work at the typewriter, with dictionary in hand, but he also kept notebooks and preserved scraps of handwritten drafts. Editing was a more collaborative process: many of his manuscripts (though by no means all) have handwritten corrections to spelling, punctuation, and syntax, which Hyatt would then incorporate into a fresh draft.

While Hyatt was initially involved in raising Dylan, he struggled to cope with Lindsay's relationship with Blond. By September 1963, he had left London, staying in Hexham in the North of England and making plans to settle there. He was soon back in the capital, however, drifting itinerantly around West London and the rest of the city for several years, staying – as he put it in a letter – 'everywhere and nowhere'. An important aspect of Hyatt's survival was the emergence of new queer social spaces. His work records cruising on the Bayswater Road, visiting the baths, and cottaging, as well as his life in the clubs and bars, resourceful, quick-witted, defiant. Though the Wolfenden Report set in motion legal reforms, the limited decriminalisation of homosexual activity didn't follow until the Sexual Offences Act 1967. The Act itself did little to improve the lives of working-class gay men who, as the distinction between public and private was redrawn, were often policed with greater intensity.

This is a neglected area of 1960s British literary culture. Out gay poets were in short supply, with Thom Gunn, following W.H. Auden's example, leaving for America in 1954. But, around 1964, Hyatt began a brief relationship with Harry Fainlight, who'd starred earlier that year in an Andy Warhol screen test, and who would make a notorious appearance alongside Allen Ginsberg at the Royal Albert Hall in 1965 (an event that Hyatt compares to fucking in a cinema in 'My Auto-Biograph Hours'). Fainlight's work – by turns explicit, melancholic, and psychedelic – clearly influenced Hyatt, and inspired him to try longer, more experimental workouts like 'Reatity', 'All Sunday Long', and 'Sh *Everyboy*'.

Hyatt had already appeared in little magazines – most notably *The Aylesford Review*, edited by the Carmelite friar Brocard Sewell – but these longer poems were some of his first to reach a wider audience. His friend Michael Horovitz, editor of *New Departures* magazine and reading series, included five poems in *Children of Albion: Poetry of the Underground in Britain* (1969), a defining anthology of the 1960s scene, dripping with references to William Blake, Ginsberg, and jazz.

By the time *Children of Albion* appeared, Hyatt was living in a small village in the North of England, with his lover, Donald Haworth, known as Atom. Again, the sequence of events that lead to this dramatic change of circumstance isn't wholly clear. In 1965, Cressida Lindsay moved from Notting Hill to establish a commune, the Old Rectory, at Scoulton Mere in Norfolk. She lived there with Dylan and her other children in the company of artists and likeminded people. Though Hyatt was welcome, this clearly wasn't what he wanted. His poetry repeatedly articulates his inability to come to terms with fatherhood and his distrust of heteronormativity, even in the radical context of a commune.

Even so, Hyatt remained dedicated to his son. Horovitz recalls Dylan and Mark 'curling up to sleep together after long bouts of mutual story-telling' and 'whooping and whirling and singing for joy' around the Round Pond in Kensington Gardens. We think Hyatt stayed at the Old Rectory for a brief period in autumn 1966 – after his release from Brixton Prison – before attempting to settle more permanently in the North. He headed first to Leeds, staying with his friend, the writer Wendy Oliver.

Hyatt had drug problems, and it's possible that, at this point, he entered or relapsed into a phase of serious addiction. His mental health seems to have deteriorated, with reports of increasingly erratic behaviour. He had already attempted suicide in London, and we know he received psychiatric treatment in Leeds. It's also possible that he was detained on a ward in Plymouth, in South West England, during this period. As a working-class LGBTQ person belonging to a racialised minority, Hyatt's encounters with any form of state authority were fraught with danger.

His archival papers – prepared after his death but reflecting his own organisation – are divided into two halves: 'Pre-Leeds' and 'Post-Leeds'. This can be interpreted in several ways. Partly, it reflects the upheaval of his leaving Lindsay, Dylan, and his network of friends in London. It also seems to register a traumatic period of mental distress.

But, more positively, it signals the entrance into his life of a new partner: Atom.

In a letter to Lindsay dated October 30th 1968, Hyatt recounts bouncing around the country, taking psychotropic mushrooms, and meeting 'Atom equals Donald Haworth', who promptly asked 'would I care bed-down at his place, I said No & changed my Mind Yes, well, well, piss-well, that's the history of the happening.' Atom would be Hyatt's partner for the last years of his life, and they settled together in a small cottage at 121 Belthorn Road, in the village of Belthorn, outside Blackburn.

This change of scene is reflected in poems like 'New Brave Wired Ones', which delights in the possibility of a bathroom with hot running water, and in his references to rustic pasttimes like drinking dandelion wine and growing peas. But the pastoral strain in Hyatt's poetry always seems to sing itself slightly hollow, skewered by what he calls in poems 'the labours of a shattered life' and the realities of 'countryside poverty'.

A neighbour, Jill Catlow, vividly remembers their 'absolutely filthy' house, and their 'filthy corduroy trousers' and 'rust-coloured rib jumpers'. She recalls Hyatt 'writing poems on the wall, on napkins, on the table, on the floor, on tissue paper, just words everywhere'. Atom and Hyatt had a decisive effect on the course of her life – 'these two gay men made me aware of the burgeoning women's liberation movement' – and helped her to break free from an abusive relationship.

Hyatt, Atom, and Dylan took a walking tour of Scotland in summer 1971, hiking for long stretches in quiet companionship. Though Hyatt worked in a miserable job at the carpet factory at the bottom of the hill in Belthorn, he enjoyed the company of local poets and activists like Dave Cunliffe and Tina Morris, editors of the magazines *Poetmeat* and *Global Tapestry Journal*, who had been prosecuted for obscenity in 1965. His work began to be published with more frequency, and he received admiring letters from poets like J.H. Prynne.

By early 1972, however, Hyatt and Atom's relationship started to break down. Hyatt was convinced that Atom really wished for a heterosexual partner and the kind of family life that Hyatt couldn't fulfil. Atom's letters to Hyatt suggest that this insecurity was itself the real problem, with Hyatt unable to trust him and fully commit to their life together. Options were beginning to run out.

By late March, Hyatt was living in a bedsit at Flat 3, 332 Dickenson Road, Manchester. It was an unfamiliar city, and he carried with him few possessions: his poems, a dictionary, a grammar book. Alarmed by news of Hyatt's deteriorating state, and by his express determination to end his life, Prynne drove through the night with his friend, the poet Barry MacSweeney. With Hyatt's permission, Prynne took Hyatt's papers to Cambridge and xeroxed them for safekeeping before returning the originals. In Prynne's recollection, the already-archaic Xerox machine kept overheating and bursting into flames.

The poet and editor Peter Baker wrote to Lindsay on April 17th to alert her of Hyatt's disappearance, explaining that he hoped Mark would show up unharmed at the Old Rectory commune and that this would turn out to be a false alarm. Hyatt had been in Manchester for three weeks, and had been 'pre-occupied, rather possessed, with thoughts of suicide'. The last time Baker saw him was the evening Prynne and MacSweeney visited. He called Atom, who hadn't seen Hyatt since April 13th. Hyatt by this time had already sent a note to Lindsay: 'Without Donald, I can't live; and being so-called free, I no longer want my "self".'

Hyatt either hitched or walked the 20 miles from Manchester to the area between the Entwistle and Delph Reservoirs in Yarnsdale where his body was discovered on April 30th. Atom broke the news in person to Lindsay and Dylan. Blond records the visit: 'I was staying at the Old Rectory when Atom came to tell us. He cradled Dylan in his arms and they both cried.' Dylan remembers Atom plunging himself into Scoulton Mere before delivering the news, then running the perimeter to dry himself off.

What happened to Atom remains a mystery. He was in possession of the originals of Hyatt's manuscripts but, burdened by their emotional toll, passed them to Oliver sometime after 1975. They were mostly destroyed in a basement flood. The undamaged material was returned to Dylan and remains in his safekeeping. Prynne's Xeroxes survive as the most extensive record of Hyatt's poems. Without their rescue, little of the poetry would have circulated after Hyatt's death, and the record would have fallen silent.

Hyatt's funeral was arranged by his birth family. Lucy and Mick O'Shea attended with John Lindsay, and remember the event as contrary to Hyatt's spirit. They travelled to the cave at Yarnsdale and read a poem in his memory. Hyatt was cremated on May 9th 1972. His ashes are interred in Streatham Cemetery in London, alongside his mother, a few hundred metres from where he was born.

The sources for this introduction come from interviews, conversations, and correspondence with those mentioned in our acknowledgments, as well as material in the public record, such as birth and death certificates and information from the UK censuses. It incorporates printed material from the private collections of Dylan Hyatt and Lucy O'Shea, and quotations from Anthony Blond's memoir Jew Made in England *(2004) and Michael Horovitz's editorial to* New Departures, *7/8 and 10/11 [Double Issue] (1975).*

—Sam Ladkin & Luke Roberts

POEMS

O POEM.

.... The arrow in the body won't fly
it remains like a stone in the sea
rolled in its own flesh
and nothing is born out of me.

POOR SOUL.

It's hard to sell loneliness
and you're going to a party.
You go cruising with good reason
like having silence in the heart.
You want a drink or a friend
to talk with. As the words fall apart
there are times you want another person
to come and hand you warmth.
From your own bitter eyes
you are so lonely that no-one understands.
The brick walls look very empty;
there's nobody about for hours;
you realise there are endless burdens
pulsing behind your hidden face.
You're of no colour to speak of
only blood, fear, and brain,
always feeling poor to the point of snap.
You say "Hello" to people
and the sounds are seen clear by someone,
then the words disappear
forever and you're lonely.
Each time you part from other people
you feel a little death inside.

YES!

Begin by thinking
they presume;
you have just masturbated
all by yourself
they know how queer you are.

They know the after-effect
of an orgasm
for themselves
so when they see you
walking bent at the knees
they know well enough

anyway the amount
of dry spunk on your belly
is unimportant
the thing is did you enjoy yourself?

Yes!

PUBERTY OF PUCK.

It's slow writing
on re-admission of the abyss
so if this body is sleepy-tired
please walk around.

Suddenly there's nothing
in the laws of the alphabet
that breaks open revealing
what buoyancy am I.

Surely the corpse of childhood
can't multiply any greater?
Only the sad hole of this new void
revisiting old headaches;

I realise the image of myself
coils round soft the life,
no longer am I wise or otherwise
but alone;

exhausted by the birth of aching,
thoughts reach me
with pangs of emptiness,
once my mind wouldn't look at,

split in thrills of urgency
growing beneath my hair,
there's somebody inside me
that wants to fight any wild space.

HASHISH ON SUNDAY.

What?
Bored with so many problems,
so many little things,
such a load of urgency.
I am a natural labourer
and I can't make one penny
into two pence.
After redundancy of the last job
I panicked, and with nothing, I wrote
off for a site on a coming local gala.
So far this is no joy ride, and I think
that I have been granted a site, for
my stall for selling gay things.
Since my last job, I have found new
employment, grossly boring, in an old
cotton mill, which now puts foam on
very cheap carpet; for me
it's a very dirty job, I come home
with rubber-foam stuck to arms, that
rubs off inside my clothes; on a normal
week it's 11-hour shifts, five and half
days, the half day is for sweeping up
the factory floor.
By birth I am a diddikai, my interest
in rubbish comes from my father's side,
and my flare of mad quick colour from
an unknown mother, unknown to me that is;
if need be I know how to lie, I was fed
with lies from babyhood to a teenager
but somewhere after leaving home, I
learned my own kind of truth.
Now at 30 years, I have a ten year old

bastard son whom I don't keep, and I
visit him once or twice each year.
I have a sad undeveloped mind which holds
a forum of dull fantasy, of rusty white
elephants, a fool's general value of most
things.
Jesus is my dog; one morning on waking up
I found he had shit all over me and the bed.
Waste of failure, less of debris, hang around
crude life, blind like a cold unround stone,
that is all of me.

"SPIRIT OF WHO'S OUTSIDE"

Spirit of who's outside
I have no secret identity
but come and sniff
my hard black sin,
it's rats under the flesh,
spider senses sucking.
The pure ugly fact is,
a load of energized shit
eating his way in space could be human.
And if you don't know what human means
well!
it's shattering

HALF BREED.

I'm half gypsy and I burn with colour
like a fat cow dancing in the sun
while dogs over the right image
play spring sound to each other
for the same smoky grass plot
being only half of a race
understandingly I know the past
and ignorance has a need to show
off the best and horror of time
half human half freak I think
of the future how sick with wine
i am in a tarty nightclub
looking into a glass of puck
feeling hell inside my guts
with dream music running
and thoughts feel all right
sometimes
what did i drink to upset my mind
that stuff called ALL WISHES
when this headache goes to poems
well i get milkman shits over Keats
being half a child of zodiac hand
i grow dirt in my ears
like a traveller's old boots
that read laments there's tomorrow
on my heals for something more
being a bit drunk i smell of sorrow
with my mouth open wide

COME INTO THE WORLD.

I miss the friends who went into their minds
  and stayed there, they put haunted horror
  on their faces, and now creep behind fired
  eyes, I don't see anymore.
I miss those people who rip the flesh off their
  bones, frighten by the truth of life, who
twist their faces into sad monster shapes.

I miss the collected eerie friends that honeymoon
  for protection from the great super-lovers
  of death, and as I miss them, I am lost
  among them in my own image

"IT'S ALL SIGHS"

it's all sighs
and know sweet nothing

about anything

all promises with acts
of indifference

all indifference comes
with all moods

all thoughts make way
over, sideways, under

to a stand-still

DELICATE.

He reads a tired book,
the book of thoughts.

He wonders at bright words:
are words like men
a shape to be broken
with a coughing sound?

He reads life into patterns,
a bursting joy in his blood.

He sees letters clear through,
print is his feed.

He fingers paper pain,
lovely.

He crosses his legs,
an action to please.

He lights up a friendly cigarette
while sight reading.

He lets senses take him,
human grace.

He turns another image,
his brains are fresh.

He draws close on his nerves
and works his body away.

He thinks on a quick visit
whilst tending his toilet.

He steals a small poem
and scars it madly.

INDIVIDUAL.

You are simply flexible
and the colours of your mind
look like feathers in your eyes,
you always chase solid facts.

You are the tapestry of much time
and you sleep like regular rocks,
in bed you are a wintry duck,
you just dwindle through my blood.

You are pale as smoke by the open sea
and the silhouette of a beautiful soft breeze,
I find you lovely as sandy headlands
on the corners of natural humanity.

PRETTY COMMON.

For many years love to me meant hurtful pain.
I could not take it, understand or enjoy
any act of love. The reason is clear now;
pride was washing my mind down to the size
of a long fat worm. Slowly I am attempting
to pore over books, also listen to people
as they actually say their words, which
in experience is limited by my dramatic
poisonous past. Before now I lived
with marvellous shadows of imagination,
that used to lead me round the twist
and leave friends carefully upset, without
another thought. I will muddle myself no longer,
for somewhere in my common human head there's
the essence of expression, to let other persons be
overjoyed that I am around to help, or made to
laugh with some silly remarks about how ugly my toes
are without a pair of socks to hide their funny shapes.
Most nights now I am alone except for pet animals,
which I like sometimes.

IT'S ALL IN THE PAST NOW.

Downstairs my lover reads stories
well into my son's brain, and he'll soon
be leaving to go back to his mother
in that flat land of Norfolk, which
is far from Lancashire, and the
young bastard will go away thinking
"How queer my father is, staying up
all night, looking in a deep trance
at nothing but unseen torches that glare
from within his large strange eyes,
trying his hand at loud lousy poems
which he can't sell to holy people."
Yet he must know, it's to know anybody
that his father is at times in dazes
which almost drive him off his rocker
with oversight with lots of things –
all without G.C.E. proof to show it.
But by now my son should be pleased
because it sounds like a great tale.
My lover reads on and my son breaks in
to question why such a word is the
word it is; How long have they been
saying that? Is my father upstairs
still in that funny odd mood again?
Is he still of common folk? My mother
says "Dad's a gypsy; so don't tell
anyone but your children, that's when
you're big enough to play the loving
lover." Downstairs the voice grows soft,
as if the story had a lovely ending.
But high up the stairs of solid stone steps
the old man masturbates the future,

trying to keep ahead. Though that son of mine remains a stranger to me, he will never ever have the fear from that deep father figure.

"IT'S DEEP INSIDE, THIS NOTHINGNESS"

It's deep inside, this nothingness
which ticks away most of time
from the quiet white-washed walls
to the downhill road,
a zombie of day and night,
without reason.

LOOKING FOR A POEM.

Almost asleep, over this typewriter,
there's very little in my mind, city-
people don't want to know about country
folk, village people talk of big city
lights, late night strip clubs with nearly
naked dancers, queers are sick jokes,
life is slow, and hours are even longer
than real time, posh people have lots of things
to talk of, and being locked up in a small
village there's few ways of make money.
Then on top of existing for death somehow
memory looks back at love and menace,
please forgive this amateur poet,
he happen to be so very sad,
no doubt you know how things are
from some point of view of your own life
at one time or another.
If I could make you laugh with happiness
I surely would, but finding words
to make things gay is not always with me,
it's very clear.

BETWEEN YOU AND HUMANITY.

My son, I am not a man that will give love,
in fact I feel you as being strange.
Some time in your life you must hate me.
All you can say is "I am from your sperm".
Breath is all I give a baby;
there may have been coal in deep winter
but I your father did not dig that coal.
Understand, son, I am a poor labouring man,
my belly thinks for me, do you see.
Oh yes! Labourers have their dreams
Not the educational type of muck
which babble newspapers pint down us
or the t.v. fantasy lust of great happiness,
but dreams of sons of the soil really at peace,
revolutionary, unknown in human history,
the courage and strength of every living being,
a way to reason pride out,
the pleasure of being able to see them as they are,
when the great game of out-witting is over,
a planet of healthy, happy, free-thinking people,
to throw ideas into the sky so fortune
falls on everyone, not the old gold family name.
I tell you, son, now, for a lifetime coming,
help share and care for someone slower-witted than yourself,
show them how life works easy good pleasure.
You may be the last of all my thoughts
when I have my moment of death,
I could, out of thinking altogether,
be at my wit's end with myself.
And as you sit beside me and want to be amused,
all I can think of is that Dale joke
about the farmer who always wore wellington boots

just in case he might feel randy, to fuck
a sheep by putting the animal's back legs
down his wellies to get to grips with the job,
and that behind going up and down the country hills
for so many years that spacemen have iron balls.
People don't want to know. I keep a clean face.
The prize of life is to be able
to eat, laugh heartily, then have a good shit
reading to yourself some soft poetry.
My son, I am not a man that will give love.

HELLO.

What shall I do?
Work all life long
until the body
out of energy
falls dead
at my feet, or
shall I tell you
my name
and you tell me
your name,
then when we are able
we could make love
to one-another
and love again.

We would get older
and older and older
until our skin
could barely go around
our bones
but
behind our watery eyes
under our grey wigs
you'd wink at me
and I'd wink back
to let you know
everything is fine
with me and you are
the one I loved way back
in them right young days
of our some time back
and still do if
I remember
right.

NEW BRAVE WIRED ONES.

we have a hot bathroom
we are going to bathe every winter now
we go to tell our friends
we are so clean you eat dinner from our tummies
we sweep our new hot bathroom out
we can't let the cat sleep there now, can we?
we laid brand new foam carpet down
we are even going to buy some posh scented soap
we like to show we think of everything
we already have super soft toilet rolls in candy
we clean the mirror every time after use
we go so far as having a fly killer in the house
we keep so-clean, clothes inside the airing-cupboard
we both take a bath together, best results, always
we don't like rubber ducks in our water
we love a real bit of each other's person
we share what we have on ourselves
we love love
we love a slap and tickle
we blow bubbles through our soapy hands
we are so clean and together
we love our dear little cottage farm dreams
we really let everything happen
we hope you'll join us in our bathroom
we only strip people that enjoy the pleasure
we hope you come
we would love you to come
we know our bathroom can hold all races at one sit-in
we only close the door to save the wind freezing our balls
we know you hate us because you are so
disgracefully dirty.

"HARK! THE DEARIE MARK"

Hark! the dearie mark
Bloody gay and salty
You'd give all the entertainment
To rise that fairy
So into control you'd live
Piss bliss to the LORD,
Champagne, champagne camp,
The middlemost clusters
And smite the bum toiled faith
Mark the deepest ass in England
The mortal mind cold in half glory
Hang on to that untamed penis
Shy as the bog god, played amazement,
Mark the trouble springs up
Then it's all quiet out of the riot bed
Listen! the jingle of Roman balls
Smelling like dying wages
Climb out and up, alltime love & thought
Plough human moods under a black clock
Reckon the hymn of rape
For a man younger than heaven spaced

Life thou art a great command

OUT OF SPITE.

Being without identity,
a separate being shared,
understanding it is necessary,
transcending sense
among unbreakable simple rules
through the deep universe of progress;
in spite of spite in spite
each fear deserves important inquiry,
driving knowledge completely beyond;
out-act the out-of-the-way guilt escaping,
show the sphere of being oneself,
surrender to love moving,
settle in nothing but death.

"THE JADE THIEVES CARVE THE WIND"

the jade thieves carve the wind
silence swings like a raffia queen
a body in bed strips sanity comic
birds wait for skies more moving
night is saving the truth
shakespeare's little girl wants
a man at his limits

THE SUN SWEATS SALT.

Country dry grass
yellow wine
wet socks in the wind
a man sleeps
children run wild —
I can't write
in the country —
a car goes past
and the sea shines.
Where is the rain?

Soon night will be here
with t.v. hours
and the poet will get stoned
on hashish
and laugh with great madness
then cry great madness.

So badly I need a trip
to the large city
and smoke.

Friends don't come
why should they?
I live out lonely dreams
and burn.
Where is the death?

Poems are so hard
yet they are very simple.
I could say:
I am a good poet!
and someone would laugh
and laugh
until their tears killed.

GREEN LIFE.

Drowsy wine, you can imagine, thoughts stand
in the distance of a rocky head, and in the lowest
region, empty ideas like barrels on a mountain
stream, listen for a loaded echo to share, the eyes
imprisoned wander through the unconquered, only
to see the invisible, I am impossible, the dreariest
dream of water locked in a cave, stuck in sneaking
corners without clean magic, just goggling.

POEM.

when cornflakes fart
boy how I sing

"BRING BACK YOUTH ROBBERS"

bring back youth robbers
driving answer cocked brightly
spread like a cat jump
starving taste

in this story my arse performs
its chief manure heap food
and you judge my public fucks
i am queen suck come to smell
shivering physician moon

to you i am death's whistling
listen wicked life
satisfy a young girl idle

voice piercing you creep
i bury you in my heart
echo you laughing by my bed
with lick comfort wedding ring

you punish me scholar
standing in chimney silence
fastened to a coffin
do you want the child i was
on a stiff pillow
reflect i am a frightened boy

hunting key holes for pity
you know I am living grief.

An empty poverty brushing along,
I am for you, lover,
glittering service, for you hurt too

We are sunset cloud crossed
by the garden of industrious tears,
you are the strange rope whirling
touches of time of tea.
We are into shit arse and soul.

"CRY BABY CRY"

cry baby cry
for the perished legend
of love
a sad epigraph of desire
body embodying body
wandering across deserted blood
while seamen sing by the coast
then madmen raise early dreams
the salt breeze zig-zags
like a snake of impressions
through a complete mood
stiff as a statue on rocks
fiery clouds in the throat
in a mosaic under the sun
a survived faded existence

QUEERS.

Pull it out and let me see it
because I like it when it's warm,
mind you, I love it, fresh,
come on, and roll with me

we can jump the bed in
and break it, doing the thing
I will lay on your back, and scratch
then just lick it up together

you can run primitive around me;
knock me over with your lot,
stuff me with what you got of it,
and I will get down, to pleasing you.

"THE MOTH IS BACK, JUST PEELED OUT OF THE SKIN"

The Moth is back, just peeled out of the skin,
naturally no perception, scabby saint, move,
abstract colour vibrations down the back, a taste
of marsh thoughts, the contemporary country
scene, hammered under the sun, the head stumbling
over squalor, find a bunk-up,

SEPARATE NOISES.

every body must dust down
the dog from the street somehow
because human kinks grow quicker
and you can lose yourself thinking

the drinking queens on black nights
put this pile by for loneliness
con this if they can

a dear little queer thinks of home as bed
and of the dirt on the earth
then thinks he misses himself dearly

how the brains boil ideas to tin cans
on the other side of greetings
a thought open into new sounds

a womb of soft voices play on light
the tap of water on water

"ALL I WANT IS COURAGE,"

All I want is courage,
To cut off the cat's head,
Then drown the parrot,
that would make me
feel better, than what I am now

"WHITE ANGELS MOVE IN THE WIND"

white angels move in the wind
naked yet each holds a half bright knife
they drift after nine at night
and try to sing people from their cottage
the land remains in a cold hush

LIFE IS A SHOCK.

living with humans is queer
they want the skin off your back
the taste of blood and salt
the sweat from pink tongue

"I CAN'T SELL MY PENIS BECAUSE"

I can't sell my penis because
it's so much littler than small
but my dear friends tell me
I've got a deep rich arse
that needs more than a wash.

All my lovers go on for better love
and I am left alone wanking shadows.
Understand me when I talk of me,
always this empty ageing body looking.

Friends leave footnotes saying "I am off"
and I am all the time there is,
asleep in a noisy city life,
wanting a cigarette to go to bed with
even a dog end would do
lavender nightmares suit me right

All the fish in the sea won't nibble me
I've got the bait that smells real poor.

HYDE PARK.

At the Serpentine,
long-haired blondy
and me
had late lunch in
a row-boat:
cold chicken & wine,
Spanish & Russian salad,
with a small breeze
and a smoke of hashish

Chop chop chop
the water against wood.
He's more of a hot pie
man, and it's —
a lovely day
for sex again.

HOW ODD.

Watching with a clearance eye
    over the health of your body
desires going through so quick,
    my hand rumbles for prayers.

You rush down my ears,
    smash my plans to decay
and like a drunk you squeeze
    the centre of my survival.

You show me black people
    living between damp plaster walls,
empty chapels in drizzle dirt
    and thin children hot with jazz,

shout at me with photographs
    about profits of foreign war
which dress the gentry on Sunday afternoon,
    then point at the poor eating their words.

You place no mystery before me
    and tell me not to dream;
with the wrath of your passionate smile
    say: "Life is all action."

Through muddy roads you go,
    talk to every stranger with problems;
"Let's share our blindness openly,
    We are in rags until we die."

There are days when you show the countryside off,
    windy early fresh cows,

twisting time back to the ancient
  gathering breath from hills.

You labour with men of twee skill,
  make the collegeboys ashamed,
nibble a monster without trouble,
  then show me industry's messy reputation.

You punch my mind with landlords:
  there are wrongs to be analysed,
emptiness explored with laughter,
  schemes on what I don't understand.

I say: "Here's a poem."
  The reply comes back:
"Get your face fucked."
  Life is more than one man's religion.

I flow behind you through Woolworth's
  and you point out the face of the crowds.
Like death you deal out questions,
  leering at me with silent breathing.

Without overtones on Cain or Abel
  you know life isn't all pleasure
but you understand film-star wax
  like a cut across a lie.

As a thought should never be careless
  you strip me of my sexy smell
and bulldoze my soggy reason, saying:
  "Your arse ain't worth licking."

Slowly you let Guy Fawkes rot;
  those games are for children.
Men reason by the reservoir,
  build with sweat earth's family house.

"What debts you owe the human body,
    sleeping in midnight of day after eating pills.
Shamed by sadness, why do you
    leave fruit to waste when you could give it?"

I whirl in my own doubt
    then you freeze into me sour dispute
"Are your trousers filled with garbage?"
    and nip my fantasy with an iron love;

"I will show you Autumn burning."
    And I watch the nature of the earth,
twenty winters and more unfold sparkling;
    you can't be false, life's not like wishes.

Local people should colour old age,
    your fantastic search is in your life,
not a moon full of holes to dream by.
    Don't ask for more.

Name me and I won't come running,
    but step out our lives together;
I will exorcize my mind over and again
    to find the famine of my bad hissing.

You will show me split reasons
    for my ruined depression
where my eyes never dreamed of grief;
    a woman clutching a friend's loss

All my goodbyes will fade;
    I've seen you sob with my stupidity
almost to a violent black fit.
    Even then, you have me wonder
        how odd things are.

TAKEN.

The room is full of fluff,
two inches of dusty fluff
to illustrate my mind.
There's last winter's blanket
on the floor behind the door,
two rusty empty coal buckets,
newspapers, clothes, clean breakfast
plates, half bottles of off country wines,
rags, belts, a mirror facing an ice-pick,
cigarette ends, dead matches, house-games;
once I lift my eyes above three inches,
fuck, what a mess I live in!
I could clean it up with some life,
but imagination stops between
thought and reason
and I let the dirt sweat it out.

BORDER LINE.

Living is worse than death
because you live
up to your conviction
with your eyes open

in death you close
your eyes to eternity.

POOR SOD.

I am getting better on my leg,
can feel my toes move with pleasure,
sense that old heart is banging away,
feel my blood roll under my skin,
in fact my body is having a storm.
I can feel the sweaty waves
drifting in this shell,
almost hear mist rising
on the inside of my skull,
a great ocean floods my head.
Yes, what lovely sounds I make
through the sea of blood;
red, white and fatty,
a little hairy on the outside,
but who cares what the surface is?
I'm greasy inside, hot and tender,
and I love it.

PUFFED-OUT.

Puffed-out, slightly sick of being;
Each day dreams get more like reality.
It's hard to know which is life, which is worst.
The head pains grow ever worse.
My mind sleeps half the rest-hours:
The clock just laughs.
I can't see what's funny
Even when I know the clock's right.

"TRYING TO REMEMBER WHAT MEMORY"

Trying to remember what memory
has forgotten or hates most.
A semi-darkness of faces
that haunts the mind with a terrible
atmosphere, silence howled into pain,
a child creeping around a house
with his shaking life, frightened and
shrieking "I'm alive."

A DEFINITE CHOICE.

I want to understand a man
And his pain,
Not the other kind of man
Who says: "I will have another
Cushion for my arse dear,
And close the door when you bring
The coffee in, while I write
An ode to mummy."

WORK AND WONDER.

I quietly work at my job
for a single poor wage
and I don't get rich like others
but have to wash with soap
to keep old day from marking me.
I am a prostitute to my city
among the daddies of this time,
on just a manly whore's income
I barely feed my lips honestly,
stupid how means are financial.
As an ageing male I snicker,
hungry money eats my life,
and I wonder
what doll creature am I
with my athletic sex?
Imagine me in a dark room alone
enjoying my own flesh,
fingering the raining night,
disgusted with who built the clock.
I have very few feelings of a man,
only ungracefully I have been trained,
my skill is respectably protected
to labour greed to God knows why.

God is control by some of the people,
a person like me is jammed.
Yes, I work under you, darling boss.
I do care to sympathetically live
deep inside my dirty shoes,
and it is on what I stand that makes me
a curled up queer jerking hours by
and in the evenings be intimate with myself.

HOME WALK.

(a poet's view of night-shift)

Six this morning, work over: now home;
the gypsy sky dark and black holds rain,
under feet the fields are waterlogged,
No poet should live at the top of a hill
and work 12 hours at the bottom, it's awful.

THIS POEM.

This is going through my head:
that we all have a killer's instinct
with our tiny aerosol fly-killers,
insecticide and petty jealousy,
each reviewing each other's flesh,
thinking on an idea of brutality;
each individual can no longer think
of the summer shaft of a forest
because trees, vegetables and fruit
are of another era,
for each person wants to strike at
the future of old memories
only because of the need for space.
The human race will move into the next universe
because it's fighting ignorance for death.
Our need will make the colour of blood our mascot
to fight the uniforms and the flesh.
The meek will inherit death
only because their shyness is cowardly.
Somewhere between here and now
we will lose the revolution
in the quiet habits of religion.
History will go blank
over the lack of interest;
we put our thoughts into machines
that will place us in a listless decadence.
The gore will stay on our hands under true man-power.
Heaven help us to birth
and the fear that's moving up the bones
like a noisy joy aiming for men;
only women will act for truth,
as all of us live in beginning of life.

It's not for me to say: you suffer.
There's a fight in every love-catch;
the human can't live with himself
or totally by himself;
each of us must look for a new cunning slaughter
and when one of us has killed another
then cut up the meat with a funny horror,
one looks at the pulsating nerves that jump about
on each separate chunk of flesh.
Sometimes one wants brutal victory,
other times there's just a need,
for something must be satisfied.
Earth is the birth of earthlings
where the Devil, the Man of God,
has lost interest under drug science.
Man puts reason to sleep, and miscellaneous flamboyance
turns the sight into musical killings.
We try to trap a wiser being into a fool;
at the same time one gives many mothers to the grave
so one can show the growing of beauty,
and how great one waits for the next charging battle,
which will lose itself only to end in a gas that will flow
around the soil of time and beg for nothing more.
Like the sound will end on nothing
but fighting words, and stop.

"WITHDRAWALS ON DEMAND"

Withdrawals on demand
the normal thing
time draws out
(of course risk is stolen)
a system that operates
simplicity itself.

DEEP SILENCE.

my bones ache with jailed
engravings of a portrait,
of a character, out of time
with the gangsters.
a man has tattooed
my mind in the tradition of
the world of the underworld,
mottoes are throned, experiences
duplicated to the last cheap
price, sensitive to justice like a
brutally beaten mute and now
and when I am candid, my
mouth remains like a prison
over my voice

"JUST WOKE UP TO A LOT OF LIGHT"

just woke up to a lot of light;
the air is so biting.

must make a large cup of tea
and go easy on the milk.

bet the postman won't call again,
must wash the lamb's blood off the door.

don't feel like getting out of bed
because there's no one around here.

it's strange sleeping all alone,
there's more to do in dreams.

A DREAM.

the bones of the finger
grip the pen to find a
poem that suits the paper
from the dark days of a tree

the pen glides thoughtless
drifting with a cold dawn wind
beside a man that walks
to a home of books

the pen is not a worker
but a sleeper of the bed
where life does not rest

IS IT NOW.

it's not great finding out
that a rich man is robbed of evil
the texture is of frustration
to shiver with a nightmare;
it isn't really nice

to crumble behind the visions,
the hearty city wit,
to wade through old commerce
for the nudity of a man.

to masturbate misty thoughts
and hold an exploding mind,
it's not great to find no person
behind the eyes;

it's harder to think otherwise

it's not good finding out
that a poor man is thinking
that the frustrations are his
and they will go with some thought;
it isn't really great

MAN BY AGE.

perverted by satisfaction;
weak from practise,
intense delight,
pleasure! pleasure! pleasure!

"SOON THE MIND WILL BE HEAVY"

soon the mind will be heavy
with mad sleep
the drug used is like a stone
that stops memories overturning
and I will be damp with dreams

experiences flutter through bitter thoughts
of a pain, on the backs of my eyes
like a leaf, with the dregs of a smile
it's like that now

GROWING PEAS.

I'm sitting here like an idiot
watching and wanting
my garden peas to grow.
There's very little to do
in a country village
other than keep it green.

Sometimes I look through
pretty clean cottage windows
all sparkling with brass
and hand-painted picked pieces
of miniature china figures
depicting days of old.
And from all this show
daily polished glory
appears a face or two
of very old people;
factories have eaten lines
beneath their eyes.
I realize they're here
to catch the youth of old age.

I'm here in my cottage garden
being pestered by insects
from all the ages,
listening to aeroplane engines
burn up the daylight.

A SHINER.

there's a window
miles away from here
catching the full blast
of a good summer
you see the shine
from where I'm
standing
Now I wonder
who lives there
so far away
from here
what do they do
for a living?
or how do they
pass their lives away?
Are they poor Irish
trying to keep
the family together?
poor jobless blacks?
wearing washed out looks
found on so many English
peoples now-a-days
My God! how that window
glows

I TELL YOU NOW.

dilly day dream
why don't you lose
that stupid bull dog pride
it's going to give you
an awful lot of pain
later in your life
dilly day dream
you better bother yourself
before you become a young man
or you're going to find
a lot of hurt inside
and the world isn't interested
in your dreamy ideals
dilly day dream
please wake yourself

dilly, silly dilly
holding onto every penny
and not caring about how your words come out
but then you say: "you've too many friends"
well! one day my silly lad
you're going to find charm ain't worth shit
and that pretty face you smile with
will be crying
and I will be sadder than ever

SAD DAY.

Slowly I lose the power to absorb myself
in stones, flowers and dreams, my moonhit brain
melting the effect of bad communication. By the
late hours of day terror grows objects inside
my paralysed head. Once upon a time
I would gather my sermons to speak
to my friends the day before they was said.
Now things have changed somewhat, most of my
intellect is spent looking for infinite death. My gaze
settles in nothing, spasms of tormented thoughts
sweat through my body til my knees move like
mad spirits. Promises, promises, that's all people
make today. Costumes fade, odours of no
direction give poor impressions of life, my touch
is now translucent, peace is falling to bits. I
think, talk, argue, is it necessary to be limited?
My human mental output is violently common
and nothing less.

FROM HOSPITAL.

Try living for a change!
But I was living
with you and the household pets
Very happy I was too
radiantly so
week-end walks across the bleak moor
the sucks 'n kisses, smokes n' jokes,
everything with you was done
on a very grand scale
I'm only sorry I didn't give you
more love

Since you ask me to kill you
my emotions are mad without music
and I can only blame myself
for what will be
the fact I will be living with the ghost of you
Something will snap in the brain
like cutting out one's confession
from the blue clear air

"THAT'S IT REALLY, NOTHING TOO BIG UNDER WIND"

that's it really, nothing too big under wind,
just looms of crazy nothings,
the very cold feet of a bad poet
the green love,
the frost only nibbles the blood while the heart
       shivers in the hill of the night,
tomorrow amuses you
I think not too good
and yesterday hurts
to be honest how can that help a fair simpleton
what's the matter with me,
I know very little knowledge of any kind
how to work from day to day perhaps
which means soft dirty jobs
that need the minimum of intelligence,
the wired way the western man lives
is unbelievable, the whole
          scented shit covered up
    in the colour of the dim
          sound of cash.
    which equals another man's life;
        – crime is that advanced –
   & used by most

DICE.

Here's to the high explosive deathbird
That troubles the vegetation on language
And separately opens the rare dysgenics
Rough like a mattock in the head!

BOOTLESS.

Poetry is a business
sold to a great fortune
for the gossip of nymphs
that breeze the town
with more dim echoes of talk
that the poet is a monster
to use language bad.

MUG'S GAME.

Seeking the rare truth
buried in a document
as if idleness holds poverty,
looking for talent
that's vice violent,
like a victim burn slow,
properly desperate.

"RATTLING FOCUS WHERE DO YOU GO?"

Rattling focus where do you go?
Between images among characters
over a recognising situation
with notorious idle benefits
influenced by the anonymous blame
(ignorant vivid hairless critics!)
paint extracts of the dazzling dead,
any attitude betrays apology,
judgement surveying provoked innocence.

Fascinating diary calls the hand
to suggestion of history glances;
uneasy fiction perfects facts
unluckily like dark loo writings.

Can a poet price tea today
with streets full of poets
and words tapestried to quick wit
beside fire on consciousness?

Heritage of hashish sea-winds
wisely ageing through the author
that sat at home on cleandoggerels
always careless in an honest night.

Stuffed with illustrated ideas
embodied in a dead living mind
oddly mixed with strange mad strength
from poppy power.

THE COMPOSER'S FINGERS.

Sad haunted strings
Courted an early days dance,
Affectionate temper
Sounds like a small wife
In miserable rain,
The nervous sonata works
Demonstrating soft force;
A faint hammer fever,
Travelling still
Almost exhausted the dead
Summer touch of yonder;
A mandolin fades delicate
Like a car under snow
On a tremendous cold terror
That lays illness in skin
When the body has no audience.

DAGGERS.

Sleep, if I could,
in sad flowers
only the eyes ache —
sing to myself
inside my skull
to the hiss of fire —
die if I could know
the science of speed
but I am never happy —
what a waste of life!
And the upsetting thing is
I know myself
to do a damned act —
laugh, if I could
but that is painful
behind the face.

SCHIZOID.

Upstairs in a body
a mind waits in hate
to split the flesh
and kick tracks
into the dear old bones;
the will can wait
on empty city streets
for a lonely person
like myself.

TAME.

I was young when I left home,
So young I had no shadow.
I climbed to my thighs and went
Fumbling for a grave,
But a stallion through silence
From one crowd to another,
Fighting nearly all humanity.
But the nerves tire the body.
Now sad and sick I live
Shut up.

A REGULAR GUY.

He closed the street door softly
into a night of a new day, bitter
clean air. Feeling very good
after a sly bit of love, a man
of many children walks home late.
At the top of the street, swinging
drunk around a lamp-post stood I.
We talked of private matters, and
laughed at the world together; friends
we be. He parted on his way, to rest
with his beautiful quiet wife. I watched
his disappearance, summer grew in
the neat stars, river water licked
the wind, around and around the post
I went, like music in a party, so
evil I was in days gone by, but
I closed the street door softly and fell
into bed with the very same lady.

WINE.

Smoke flowing out of the hill
Into a sky dry of raindrop,
The landline bright white in heat
and sun too hot to look for,
Only the sweat of country light.

A country wine clouded to gold
And shadows become moving dreams
For humanity blood-coughing liberty.
Wine, wine for the head to make
More clouds in history!

Hurrah!
Away with carnival day
And the sweet ache of old wine!
Nothing can happen in the country.
Down with the sun and up with the rain!
Wine, more dank wine!

INCONCLUSIVE ENGAGEMENT.

Rolling my eyes up another hill
through new green grass
and hoping to count all the stones
half hidden in the ground
as odd animals run out of sight
and my bones ache with roots
on a star that hangs in the head
with steel wires right through
the blood of a man looking
at an open ripped bodyless lamb,
quiet sound penetrates a pain
which runs in the damaged torso
as last year's leaves hold on
to this spring's trees
and a farmer lets a shot-gun
bang like ice tongs grabbing air
while excellent slang
crowns a tear of senses
to harass a fire-torch torture
with a fighting bull inside.
A broken skeleton, a bird sings —
the whirling energy ships
carry unfaithful teeth
fairly drunk, cold.

"TWO QUEERS LIVE ON A HILL"

Two queers live on a hill
drinking home-made wine
and dancing around the cat
until both are quite ill.

We got hash and cash
and the wind is fucking cold
that blows down the country road
but the night cries get smashed

He knows that he's sweet
understand it's salt and spunk
everyone thinks of bed
and in dreams nothing is complete

please, another happy record
for I am sleeping under my face
burning one of those god cigarettes
which I need so much.

"LOVE IN THE SHADOW OF SUMMER"

love in the shadow of summer
hanging low on the carpet
The walls are so bloody white
And love might have a hangover
The music is bitter like wash water
Where do the shadows go at night
is it into the mind of everybody
or do minds hide in the W.C.
And wish of stars of rot
Can we humans think of more tricks
No eyes on my face
I don't want the heat that brings sleep
for all my sheep don't jump
my sheep sleep in dead winds
love's feet are bouncing on the floor
The soul is resting in old Hell
Must catch up with time on the clock
Also I got to drain my penis of life
it drops down with touched days
How about fucking life silly
just for fuck's sake

POEM.

I have to feel for words
Like pains on time
Like plans that colour wrong
Such as love gone insane
On a blanket of order
Somehow I am about to live
In death of the trees
Death is all I eat
And I am man.

SO SO.

I have kissed the birth of death
on a man of my own blood
and I did not care for my own action
as the body was dead and the day young
so was I but never thought about then
if I am hard like a season out of date
then who ever I am with feels strange
and I look bitter.

OF SOMETHING ELSE.

High by a small waterfall
smoking a joint to bring
the sun out of the remains
that winter has left behind
in the dead gold of fern
which hangs down one hillside
below the unleaved trees that
drop out of the wet black earth
branching twisted over
the droppings of moor sheep.
On the way from the cottage
to this place on the page
I picked up a sheep's skull
and a shadow of a bird
made me jump as it flew through
empty branches.
This grey-white head frame
now lying before me
shows me the age of myself,
intoxicating pictures
stripped by consciousness
have started to spring in colours
so freshly gay like an idea
of a prolonged sleep
at length with a lover
on the longest dimension of love,
as now the sun has lit
this paper, while an insect
with six legs and two of something
else examines another object
and I listen to the rush-rush–
rush of wind over water,
dry like a dot fly.

DAZZLE: LAMENT DIAGRAM.

Nightmare disturbing existing impact;
an obsessive idea numbs the future;
this my destiny is betraying: nihilism,
frighting development (Don't make the mark!).
This strange object — my mind —
can't stand the pain of your humanity
(curious cluster-void eats quiet explosions,
senses experience's infinite stunning meanings).
These hostile wars that hurtle through you —
begging unearthly emblems of help, bone-club-wise,
fearing this fantasy of human hopelessness
in this conventional escape-adventure which
shows the mind's state — are juxtaposed beautifully to
the truth, and entail surviving alone, the fault being mine.
To this head, it is better to be lost rather than
feel lost of intelligence. What is mind? — designed —
this chewing dialogue body is battling over:
can it walk without its ancestor-image,
and be good to culture losing its old backwardness?
This personal revolution is blowing the thoughts
aggressively striking the brain into life.
Naturally, you're weak to this glossy audience,
but image yourself reborn to go shatteringly-transparent;
but simply understand: my self-destructive
nature won't hold out for evolution. Fearing the loss
of my greatest support (that is, chillingly, you),
unconvincingly I look both ways for you around,
only needing twisted safety.

POEM.

rip
i lack you
queerly

THE DAY'S SAGE.

The eternal day breaks out
into a gaze of peaceful winter;
the country lies like an angel
with unfinished colours singing
in mist of weeping dust;
cold clouds fixed like prayers
beyond the obeyed land; the sky,
blue with the darkest pain, simply
hovering; the sympathy wind
dancing like a child out of senses,
the day commands triumphant.
Life trails the air in recitals,
feelings sing enjoyment constantly,
the throne of light falls to earth,
glory parting harvest to mankind.
Old time rehearsing like a lady,
sounds grow without discipline,
joyous be the little home in the morning.

"FROM THE POOR FREAK STREETS COMES A LAD"

from the poor freak streets comes a lad
that turns intellectual over a soft art
and meets all the big bohemians with cash
so the poor lad thinks again about things
and if he went independent on free crime
the uniform he uses might glow a little more
so being an octopus old-timer day robber
time seemed to slow down nice and easy
and the more rich people he met by chance
in sweet thatch houses he slowly got more money
the wine poured better to each new face
just like the ruff of a rabbit he stood out
he always had a quirt in the side pocket
to make the birds sing like a gorilla
and every hand went to the bank with prayers

JACK'S UNION.

flowers
pink, black, white

black, blue,
singing

"I HAVE DRUNKEN THE BROMIDE"

i have drunken the bromide
and still the night is unusual
i enter footprints in my head
and the rain is shimmering down
the room is more like a ladder
and i can not move my body
ghastly things track the mind
and nothing is happening but
the colours of objects are filtering
the carpet grows to the window
the rooms stays madly quiet
i must lie down right now as
death must come casual

"LET HIM GO IN MIND"

Let him go in mind
and he pushes lovely strokes
to the bottom of the flesh
making each sensation rhythm.
His masculine ribs move
like a reflected mirror lying
strongly feeling want him.
He is a man and shows it.
Beds roll in your eyes like walks
that urge you to be symbolic
of cradled nipples.
Lazy relaxed across his body
you dip a shoulder forward
to bring him out standing.
Will you spread the position?
Love reaching the face trapped
                until you act in sex,
you are wrapping up to him
in a gay sensitive fashion
like a dog out for the night;
you are bending into marriage.
The attitude could be satisfactory
so let him undress you to pleasure
and maintain a powerful embrace.
By male time he is coming, desires
your natural love so easy,
he is your understanding tenderness.
Of course sex is making love,
and your mind holds up between work,
or exciting intercourse on the floor
because you want to feel possibly
the female on his tongue,

pinching him where it hurts pink.
You're a woman for him,
ain't great lovers marvellous boys?

"ORAL PICTURES OF LOVE"

oral pictures of love
quite physically mental
to satisfy stimulating health
overwhelming the orgasm beautifully
hanging the breast on lips
rewarding soft body quivers
moist experience to pleasure
between legs engulf the strength
worship the strange squirms travelling
the body thighs carry happy
the ejaculation of ecstasy
a husband's nature explores another male
like a girl arouses society
kissing a male's deep history
enjoying the sight of intercourse
co-phenomenon electrifying the feelings
tingling with vital life
the walls of the penis is visually warm
undressing the body physically nude
surrender like a boy for sweet delicate hurt
night is sex for her man's girl boy
lubricating stiff partner comings of contact
muscles squeeze the full image
the mind realises   the body wanders
the touch zones adjust their energy within
lover limp with hands
on nervous gentle blood laziness grips
automatically the tight orgasm
goes up in explosions   slipping magic

BREAK MY NAME.

I, thinking of a loved one
Deep in the heart of sleep
Climbing dreams through strange bodies
And trying inner love-places
Where rest is a waste of life,
Am coming to an idea
That love is work of always
Crying baby joy.
Morning is under every eyelid
And I, thinking of his thinking,
Know a little pain
That hangs on his skin.

"HEY GOLDEN LIMBS"

hey golden limbs
i see you have had it
that edwardian shampoo
and i just love that
hair net darling
it makes you like beauty
fading into nobility's

face facts

MOON TUNE.

like a boy sprawled out by night
harping on the sky that is wild

NOTHING TO DO BUT LOVE YOU.

loveyou like a pyramid of boys
swoon with sorcery in the lounge
jig like a gorilla in dust

"A HIGH HEIGHT WHEN THINKING"

a high height when thinking
and the time is everso cold
you help a lady of the night
make a few friends outside
and they all put on a mask
as you wonder where mercy is
when words are like moving mansions
from destruction and banishment

COUNTRY POEM.

The coming of the sun
  through cottage windows

The day is crisped

The pussycats hang around

The day bus goes by all red

The young children trip along
  to school that's down the hill

The country is bird quiet

The recordplayer sounds low
The sky moves blue to blue

Through this wide-awake daze
  the body sways to the fire

The season is still under winter

The senses are happily light

The wall on the other side of the road;
  those old stones look very cold
    through this morning's brightness.

The best a poet could do is state
  the softness.

HIGH BLUES.

yes to you and no.
it's terrible how I balance
on the exhausted song
in a thrashing cold wind
when you are not at my edge
I rise by night a giant
that stands in your face
and broken dreams fly out
with teeth settling
under your heart like a poem
fresh in a sick personality
deadout on a raw vision
to shake a fist of awareness
sensitive to mount a name
that's out for a lark

"NOW I LIVE IN THE NORTH COUNTRY"

Now I live in the north country
but now and soon I have to go
to London for the trips you know
I smoke with friends and get smashed
only my mind is on the look-out
for someone who is a mad person
who walks the night streets
hoping to find me really alone
yes he lives in a deserted body
and puts labels on anything beyond him
his concrete words fall into dirt
and he knows how he lives
by the punch-up culture he wants
when possible he is going to knife me
somewhere in the back of the city
I will tell you now
he can't bear the queer touch
it is not in him to reveal
that he is the amusement of madness
so I must eternally watch out
for his hand is after my life bitterly
to me he's like a shadow of a smell
and I wait for him to come behind me
he will do it that way because I know
what's in his stillness
I won't change the skeleton I live on
someday he will place a few indentations
into my face like footsteps I understand
but I have a gun now to burn him out
or lay him out of order over the hour
and very deep in his resting bed I walk
for him waiting on the ever ready

while he casually washes himself in blood
just like the man of the poet
he dreams I will be bulging in great pain
that he dressed me in while he looks
and I wait upon the moment

K.Y. POEM.

tree Autumn
to paper sadness
not a mouse –
moving sound
only Atom

SO MUCH FOR LIFE.

Silence is duty to support freedom,
you must dress yourself anonymous,
for under the loitering quiet
a fear roams home before you think.

You fret wild crystals out of skin
to hide in a sense you know is wrong,
standing erect in a lengthening face
that can barely hold the fright muse.

Silently you close some life to revolt
and forfeit a tiny stored dominion,
as the dearest of what you remember
must never be spoken even to tree boughs.

You pluck grief from self corruption
and rest in the midst of the journey,
then ruin your lips with well spent glue
moving in pangs of modesty like a frame.

To support freedom duty is silence
and you're not worth a word of city talk:
you forsake the winnings for waste:
in true woe the tongue must go dead cold.

TRUE HOMOSEXUAL LOVE.

I stimulate solitude to satisfaction
and practice different masculine emotion
around an unfinished boy adolescence.
These masturbation interests are not
fashion, only lonely parent methods coming
out of a truly beaten boy from the past.
If anybody cares to study the habit I use,
rub up all the childhood experiences
I lived for the feminized role one had
to behave in front of domestic partners.
Early life exercised makes orgasm almost
impossible to escape with genuine joy.
Even as a man I still move under the shadow
of a woman's belt or a father's wooded plank
which displays effectively in the madness
I close, mounting the love one excites;
between beings I try to lose aggressiveness.
I had harsh punishment to become a legend
giving birth to one's lover's personal myth
and hope I resemble the source of the failure;
opportunity prostitutes itself once for love
for the active achievement I have resulted with,
the lovely-man I let intercourse the body
feeds a marriage affair and successful freedom
which I consider serious legitimate love
until adult parting doom. But here's the truth:
do I love love?

DEAR FRIEND GO AWAY, PLEASE.

Because I have an English poem
in my lap, of green-wooded sex,
I think somehow I must try
to find a mother's want in me.
Please, dear human friend, go away
from this gore of shyness
which bears in great silent agony
a need for you,
but think, in under-understanding this,
all this is me, dear brains
showing clean how simple how reason,
the pilot tiger of bitter nest,
feels I am a man maiden who
really looks silly
when this man bothers with another man,
and speaks plain horror
only to upset my friend's thought
into what my deep mind feels it comes to
for you to clear thought.
I don't know whether pain thinks pure
pain inside your insideness
but I love you in pain,
also through anonymous hellish agony
without you, my man believe me,
but I will lay down this letter law
somewhere in the hurt that settles in me.
If I ever think of you somewhere
where you are not without your image,
I will allow you to forget me,
because I am selfish to forget
every minute just past through the head
which is coloured to death,

to find myself in the lies I live
though pot-headed or pilled to sleep.
You live as my childhood horror
of something-stranger I could want fantastically
I did try to be from the early dream,
you are the horror I am looking for about me
with these pick-fingered words
that fade after death.
Please, dear friend, go golden,
without one fear of me.

NERVES BLOTTED OUT.

If you are my lover that pulses sperm
into my word crazy unbusiness-like head,
you will see how educated I am by tragedy
and how I spy at hate only to stand up,
but I will not be wounded by someone else's
endless triumph which dies mean.

You are my lover that fathers my womb
and polishes the ghost of my coward soul;
you only murder my face at the window
then hold my skin up to show street friends;
you stagger over me like an artists' rage
then clean out my belly, pounding kisses on me.

My lover, you let the wooziness of brutal love
zoom along my body, squeezing stars out,
and I let you throw rotten apples in my eyes;
you make me go squirming through your bed,
but don't feel awful, because I do let you
laugh as you brush fur under my feet like weeds.

I see you as my ruin and within me the life.
As you spray the flesh with hot sparks
I hurt and howl then scream in hooked horror,
but I would never let my legs run from you:
I may go to hospital dressed in your answers,
but you are the gorilla I love to play with.

My lover, you are with the tides of mud
that splinters my marrow with skullful pain,
but you and I are like that, without nerve.
In the masterpiece of your classic life

I remain the crushed pygmy of spirit season
the wild queer dressed up in freakish ideas.

If you are my lover and choke on whirlwind
blowing the dust of blues from your armour and
spit up the left-overs of experience like a servant,
well sometimes I am touched by mutual mistrust
and the poverty of my head will tongue a snarling.
But my pawnshop love will stand each inch beside you

beyond the late hangings of life.

this is a terrible bit of writing
famished of face and no questions
it is just a graveyard for the eye
language seriously frozen over
to make the obstacle an impassable laugh
experience is narrowed to morose tangles
travelled words stumble the whole trip
which is only wild air that is strained
no struggling motto summit to go to
died ideas cover the naked land threshold
the poet is defeated to the cheekbones
on a sting slippery tight failure
for the sounds wearily totter on weaker
shivering to a silent crawl to perch
below a mist of panting silence to be sure
the distance will be death with violence

EXTENDED MOVEMENT.

When you are lurching alone in a room
and you're in a love-made fabric whisper,
the exhaustion on the heart could be endless
like twin shadows with original ribbons
coated in flowers of the dark ages.

If you dream of knowledge calling to you
with a democratic merit like companionship,
making your feelings tender as of hesitation,
and you have a question of natural silence
with an unbelieved truth by human standards,

if you criticise all praise really correct
and you look like the triumph of agony nodding,
then the only thing you do is firmly wonder
why you out of everyone have an anxious mission
in the strange city in the book of years;

then you feel the teeth clatter like music
or emergency knives around the world.
Genuinely you look for help in any form
and delicate as you are you're not fully complete:
you hang over a prickling machine very heavy.

Needlessly you glance at life's brilliant seasons
and you have got to shock the fantastic dictionary;
somehow you want the power of lovers in darkness:
all you do is go wailing at the mind that is broken.
And your hand has no writer's method for hiding

"I LOVE MY ARSE TO BE SUCKED"

I love my arse to be sucked
it makes me come awfully nice
and I stretch the body open

....

you and today's fixed fantasies
report you are bored by shit
that's because you're fucking weird

....

you write ugly poems to death
and you are a whore for words
you're a lovely tragedy

....

balls on your stupid words
have games with your bloodless wife
and let imagination go

....

now if you really care
and honestly understand
then gently die

BETWEEN CHAOS I COME.

In dreams of sleeping pills
I could sit for eternity,
let you take the mind away
in the destruction of death,
and, in a centre inside
the body, could grow so cold
as you open my only grave
I think my mind could not care

"DESERT BONES"

Desert bones,
a dossier of a victim,
perhaps a brilliant archive,
they could be just that:
the grey flannel prep school
boy that passed with a degree,
punished by a dream
in this whirling cold fear,
lays the author
with his tycoon will for words
how this intimate age –
flooded the writer's life –
is beyond the sound of thought.
You see these bones gained nothing
from its civilization,
only the chaos of large nightmares,
in this hand-typed murmurings
the body wrote horrifying images,
maybe near the end like stories,
but bursting with a public disaster
that lived under an overwhelming pity.
One feels the wind take a show
right through the real lifetime,
now I tell you what's in the mirror:
the mistress dances lost in the head.
If you people look at the letters rolling
before your sound eye you will see
how the poet of this poem is a labourer,
seeking some silent future
for the miserable havoc career now.
Never did I demand a stir of satisfaction,
only now can I let myself go,

and demonstrate the only flickering object:
I focus myself under my face:
the super youngish electric man I am stands
for the mess of this poor great message,
stands up only for you placidly.
and those the brain crumbles into dust air.
My younger lover records something happy,
looking over bones that laughed in mutters
which hurt him dreadfully,
but he loved me with or without my care:
I really hope he will want to die beside me,
only I demand the truth to him.
For phobia strings us to beauty
under the last look of touches which turn us
into imagined crawling desire.

ONCE I DID THIS.

All I want to do
is only to do it,
don' feel like hanging
on to anything,
only to get down
to the bottom
and do it right,
break it clear.

SH *EVERYBOY.*

The Clown stares at me
　　　　　as if I made him
　　Two broken eyes
　　　　　　　Coal-black & Steel-cold
Sad He is
　　　　by the cold air around him.

Moon-head
　　　think
　　　　　I've no answers
　　　　　　only a mind pickled in blood.

Clown
　　I see the War-Face
　　　　　　Hiding behind shadows
　　I feel fire
　　　　　in burnt eyeballs
　　　smell gas
　　　　　　what a way to play
　　I know you're trying to drug me
　　　　　　into war.

Come clown orbit through my head
　　　　　if my head is large enough?
　　　　　　I change in the Light
　　　　　　　　sweat & spin
　　　like black-ravens
　　　　　　　– caught in a cob-web
　　　or whip me with age
　　　　　But
　　　　　Accept through your mind
　　　　　　I've no visions.

No-Lovers
    No-Bombs
        No-Air only me
        I am being filtered by choice.

Why Narcosis when I am thinking?
    Its sleep upon knowledge.

SMOKED.

It goes through the body like a satellite
        because one wanted it that way
                holding back a mouthful of air
                        trapped in the tears of doom.

Looking at the most beautiful thing in the universe
        known in the dictionary as a human;
                what is it in these eyes that burn?
                        the knowledge of tragedy.

O let time spin around this mind right now
        & the liquids of these eyes be forever lissom
                because the substance of the mind feels like lead.

The same old blood runs on, in crime-philosophy
        digging the aged invisible kick
                to put one's-self on an electric grid
                & fray with years.

I hope the war in the apple-orchard ends soon
        for all the missiles I've are filled with love
                and they will drop like birds from the sky
                        on the drawings of desire in this heart.

ANSWER DON'T MOVE.

I see artiliery friends evaporate
into lousy night trips,
they can't murder me
for fear.
Benches of cowards
calling:
pretty queer;
they know their own voices.
I fly my dreams
& motorbike lovely sweet heaven
looking for my own dead.

We're coin pretty,
Lovewish,
Absolute devils on earth.

Treat me carefully
because I am bleeding truth
and that shit.

You want what I want, bastard.
You're after my life.
You twisted snot…
picking out the gold.
You're not silly but I am, somewhere.

Queer little things
I think you are only human joys
but of you of me:
Little coward hello,
Looking down the corridors.
Yes, I am coming

like water on a desert
to feed the hopeless
and the lost
but they are small in number.

I will drag your motionless life.
Across hell with me
into the dark fear called mind.

ELEEMOSYNARY.

I spread the Latin wings, a Moth, dressed like
a hairless rat, heading for a grain of light,
exposed to your fear, a mere figure of sound,
the tax-gatherer to Judas, in a pilgrim's
fight around the asylum, its one phenomenon to
another, the virgin composing a language,
neither in paradise or the nutshell of knowledge.
Mark this well, my rare courage of leprosy is
not from the empire of defeat, but the blacksmith's
hours of leisure, I am out seeking to entice,
holy nice pride that's buried in the sands, no one
astonished, and enter friendly conversation,
saintly like, nearly killed by a debtor, am I
the damned tormentor? Out for the infernal
banquet, a feared king of darkness, fat on
fragments of huge committed mankind, violent with
my shadow, a countryside poverty, the desperately
fallen marriage of laughing-shock, the unmasked
documents about the rendezvous, freely lavishing
on a lady's honour, meanwhile the years go on, the
triumph of the spectators, flogs on sight.
The jugglers work below on small talent, in the
human legions, out to kill, me with my adventurous
deeds, there's no intermission on any vice, the
idleness of wealthy knowledge flies, teeming with
sad shepherds, beginning to end, chilled relaxation
with an emperor's heart, the victim of a curse, a
devil's stench, hitting the wall again and again,
flying this dangerous journey, erected by night, a
horrible tempest, this my imagination transforms down
the court, one day in the dead, another fashioned
by the custom of hell, of foretold future, without

the rank of a wizard, an angel in everlasting bliss
praised by punishment, this wicked necessity to journey
with my cloak and secret sight-seeing, past a
numberless count of heroes, forced by the fiends,
sometimes burnt by jealous heretics because of an
arena with its multitude of visions, their
utter ruin, others possessed nothing.
Now I am flying towards the experienced champion,
and I am stuck in the middle of a cob'web, soon the
beast will come down and suck my body, a sunbeam
will bring confusion, it must be the adversary, the
task of conquering must be choice, wrinkled and bent
she comes, this queen engages the gigantic circus
crowds to recognize the enemy, with promise and pledge
she comes forth, dragging her injections of new tortures,
its got to look like this, one passive and suffering
moods, the active, singing on the hour of conception,
making eyes at the subterranean Pluto of Liverpool,
intimate bonds fall like fortresses of opinion, it's the
same practical joke played by every other saint, the
modern Babylonian greed, thinking youth concealed a
treasure, but youth holds the very thing Solomon placed in
a vase, to avoid publicity of pop delusions, my killer is
a friend, unable to make any answer, it's the on-lookers
that slash the mind, for death.

ALL SUNDAY LONG.

A knife
hits my back-bone
as a sparkling boy
puts wires
through my head.

Through.
A cold steel hammer
beats on my chest.

In the cracking up
of my body
my organs are being sorted
by master eyes;
as a shadow walks into life
and purple colours.

I move
cold as a fish in hell
shaking my body.

And again, the boy
combing my body
with an electric comb.

My eyes long to fall out.
My lungs are loose at the ends
as I am;   disappearing
I go into two pieces
or more;
pains of me; jumping
into stiff pains.

And madness is setting in;
   now I am crying
     and I don't exist
       but somewhere in my past –
       I must have felt a need for me.

ELECTRO-MAGNET THINKING.

The great slaughter of tranquilizing is on; I am dictating
the ancient pharaohs to master the blindness & so
hashish-lovers of pickled-worlds the organisation must be
obeyed or you'll finish-up missing from the universe and the
entire system is highly developed in this open empire
our digestion for insight is prehistoric & poets are like
horizontal-skeletons of history; we're a dinosaur in our-own-
womb & ministers of the night throw stones at us & we hold
a great sphinx in our slums to watch pennies; magic-money
which flies back to the rich; the monster-minds are out baby
& we're up to our telephones as serious-demons play with
visions mapped before our choice but the crystal-ball is
buzzing as we crawl into death; wooden-doctors fit us to
orders & the great ritual is controlling our best acts.

REATITY.

For Harry Fainlight

Ice-blue is love under everything dying
     & ice-blue is over the bars

it's a level & —
        the only shot through one's own life
and all one desires.
  I am, as always, in front of a mirror
without any reflection for vision;
     I am so dry of love
        and so old in reatity
like a bird dying in the wind
     kissing the tears of pain.

        Sounds drift through me
           like knives of coloured blood.

Ice-blue hit me; and felt my dreams;
     & all things breathe air.

Early hours are warm
          with self-desire in every pit
     my hands & legs are so far away
        I've no blood & everything is bright
     I keep burning in my throat
     I keep dying in reatity
     I hear light in feelings.

It falls like a cloud of mist
   ice-blue is biting
      Like sweet children boiling inside oneself
       rainbows in lines of light;

There's no holding onto ice-blue
ice-blue shakes each chamber
and spins all rain-drops in mid-air

is there any sense?
drifting up and down.

Ice-blue is blood
the sounds of life again
back to dawn.

Cars are running through the light.

Even my eyes have eyes
one can do all but which truth rules out
one can do all which truth can do
one dies for it in the end
oneself rocks the very blood of flowers.

All night
the beauty is rolling in
for in me there's much dry pain
like silver.

I am seeing
and I feel as if I've loved many bodies.

LYONS.

A plastic top table & a jar of sugar
dead centre an ash-tray
shadowed by a river of smoke
    (Feminine or Butch / it's a developed love).
    or
Known & seen
two pairs of hands stroke opposite sides
of the dividing line;
                nerves count time
pics in the eyes feel
straight in front the door of all life
a new essence of afar treasured being.

He is warm as a recent discovery
    & is needed;
                like things from Hell
almost all human-minds don't see;
a spearhead of sick air
    forces every tender move
& builds his cell of human-torture

Two eyes connect two eyes;
                rebounds love;
the spell holds as he's myself
nothing is feared in the split;
                good-bye
"see you some time"
                in the wind on the face;
I am with him like bottled air
    until I break.

RADIO-ME: THE BIG SEND UP OF EVERYTHING AROUND US.

If You ever find out I am in love with you
         & you see me running away like a horse with its ass
                         on firc
          it's because I've no more of me left inside
               & words won't keep the world together.

If I am staged or child-like
               to my fellow-man
then it's because there's no affection
                  between us.

I buy sweets for young children
             because I can't cope with them
     and for teenagers I talk in dreams
     to give them hope; for something better.

When I buy an old man a cup of tea
            it's for the same reason of being lost
     and when I make love to a dog
         I try to forgive myself for not understanding.

On desiring fruit in display on market-stalls
         I remember that all beauty will come to decay;
once being forced to kiss a dead man in his coffin
        I had hatred for living such mockery.

Now & again I fall in love with women and lose my mind
        but she always belongs to another & I never touch her;
I've no need to sleep with women
       they have their own beauty.
          Now and again I love myself
    and wonder what part of me thinks the most.

On picking flowers of nature, and not the state
      it's to show I care for humanity, not the laws of man;
   in devouring a friend I lose myself for love of him
    but this friend is like money; he comes & goes.

More often I kill the desire in men but return it
     sometimes I bite at their mind's structure & get hatred;
  then like the wind I do my rounds & bring home their dreams
    & I am blessed like an animal that speaks english.

"RE-REFLECTIONS SEASON WEAKER"

re-reflections season weaker
a new kind of man —
holds this sanity together
in a spring of heat,
old fashioned by standards now
but suffer-less for more
separate self,
knowing this being could be
absence to death
only luke-warm like a statue.
in these bones are naked flowers
slowly growing, unseen
to old human eyes that knew
what this body stood out for,
this man has glued —
almost nothing of life together
back tracing atom to atom,
inside a bye-gone is dying
and a baby man starts on life
at this moment it looks sick,
and sometimes pukes
out a heart of habits for good,
this finger writer
may read like a solid monk
going into rages of sadness
only this reflection is drained
of solid sad amusements,
this body is very cold in the first
winter of maturity,
but the cold will go by the way
of will alone.

LOVE LIMITS HISTORY.

fuck beyond existence
space swept victory?
BEGINNING to word
the vanishing holds,
humble until strong
then fly out of the master
without war-pains,
mystery living still.

BORED.

Death
– creeps
like men into silhouettes
& rots
quick as friendship;
                    jerking a memory;
                            shapes & voices
          into a truth.

O Nothing;
          the mind masturbates
the scrapes of war
     coughing on society jokes
          trapped & exposed.
Death;
– bites hard work
          & perhaps the will fails
                    to learn;
                            cares drift
          as people talk to the old image
               innocent they submerge;
                    and emits a margin of smells.
death
-disarranges this world
          by time & money.

MY AUTO-BIOGRAPH HOURS.

1

It's like
shitting in a dustbin
with the lid on

Dark
Warfarin hot
air
smells masturbation

Shapes
drifting endless
under films
coloured

Packed
every hour
like the Albert Hall
on June 11th, 65

One –
slides in
like
fresh air

Gently
sits in sighs
& sounds
satisfied

2

Shoulder
to shoulder
sperm falls
from the seat behind

Down
in the front row
someone
sleeps
in methylated spirits

Every –
eye sees one young boy
& a man
playing with life

Hollow
the head counts time
a new partner
one feels virgin
like the first time

Nerves
or need, the knees knock
until still
as a yew tree

Tingle
a touch of tinsel
as a hand
tips the top of the knee
desired

3

Slow
the grey dry hand
moves
down the leg
& gropes around
the prick & balls

Unzip
go the flies
pat pat over the underwear
into the entrance
& hair

Out
comes one's-own flesh
backwards & forwards
hand, prick, hand
nothing

Under
goes the hand
& the index finger
shoots
into the ass

Balls
whirl in the throat
desire
sperm flies out
energy drops

4

Wet
the hand
rubs the sperm
back into its own hairs
& dries its-self

One's
own hand is pulled
onto the other knee
& down the leg
onto a ready stiff prick

Up
down
in time to the pic
goes the hand
with a shapeless –
well-used prick

Beat
the balls
with a smile
from the partner
in fixed hope

Dead
like squashed maggots
he shoots
which smells like –
one's-own rot
of the mind

"THE WORLD IS AT WAR"

The world is at war
what a waste of sex

FROM MY FATHER TO ME.

a loving, a thrusting thing,
a fighting urge to kill time,
the love lesson of life
compact
in a ball of gleaming power.
that was I
who came hopping into history
another mark in time,
I took my leave of a nice warm womb.
after all the time they had waited
they expected me to smile –
I cried.
my father looked down on me
and said:
I think he will be a coward
and I will hate him for knowing that
I am his father.
So clear were his words
so hard was his look.

TO MY MOTHER, DEAD.

Nineteen years all dead
deep under this appointment of life.
Your bones were made to rot, like love,
because no two people can live
a life-time together and say
'we have enjoyed every moment'
And if heaven is for the dead
life must be hell.
Bless your soul, my dear,
for I pass away in human sleep.

And did you not know
his love would not last?
For men are beautiful and bitter
as the earth
divine with their downfalls
like death at birth.
I pray, let your past be past,
for unhappy blood
can stick like mud.

POEM ON MY BIRTH.

bare leaves
fingertips raising silver hair
rotting
like old petals
dropping keys
the blossoming sky blossoms
hides on death
but hints at man's object
crash
comes a crying baby's body
away
out of its mother's sugar blood
little bull
that made a man's sufficient pride rise
mild morning
the horn has made a herb
carving
another empty space
the distant knot awakes
naked around its edge

a basic body
wrapped
in cool ocean cotton wool
an intelligence
wed-lock socket
gleaming fat
from father
white flakes fog and fill his body
silence breathing
a flicker of a voice
maybe the seal of a happy chain

unwanted, unanswered for
a leaping echo of unknowing actions
two bodies cross
making a deep dim three.
set me a beginning
for an outpost
for politics or for needs
a mirror
upon the man's head,
the wit
and a humble use of power
of my father.

"I TRIED TO LOOK FOR A BODY"

I tried to look for a body
to take home to bed
for the warmth of another body
and to have more legs under the sheets
to feel love pressed upon me
and to let the axe of time jump out of me
or to let dirt and desire do their best
to restore my mind.

FREEDOM IS A WASTE OF PAPER.

I feel the yellow-heart dies for sanity but my
exile mind has no roads; I find no hours and I
try to shake myself away from dying sleep.
My desires are air as shoes walk in my body for
pain but I am incapable of rest; as peacocks sing
my death I am out in shapes & letters are my gold
but pain is the god of the mind.
Kiss the lover for the hope of seeing.
Planes kill the child for pleasure and I am given a
bubble to box with; by the romance chief of law like
my dead lover held all beauty; also I am left to
butterfly around the taxman in exchange for the business
of living; can I weed out a few thoughts that would
kiss masters and I don't think spears could bring out the
birds of peace because even fish have to hide.
I still look for the non-stop-mirror that could hold
one mask with horrors playing the words of doubt.
I vanish even into an investigation without the war-lords
of my country starting on my name & the doctor of paints
whispers for my soul but I hold the power to
cruise my mind.
I will trade yesterday with to-morrow and only the lush lever
of insight will I trust with my bones until
all war is over.
I give my voice away if I could but it alone is lost
in the riddle of existence then looted.
Ego is mother in all matter and needs a strong lover
to act free-father for the coming of sons as new yokes lose

the goal; I see; we the dead are near.

My bones are hollow but know the labours of a shattered life
and old age tells me: to end the endlessness of expense.
Colours hold no reason; & a thousand copies of me looks
for knowledge; around a negro wish & how I jump reason
I will never know.

I whisper horrors and peanut-pains give no disaster
but dry out my skull.

a match shows my guilt by its darkness
as I see
my shadow wants my death.

AWAKE.

For Wendy Oliver

    Gypsy
        talk the language of fortunes;
    swift as the griffin
        over the plexus philosophy
    where the pains stay
        in the head of humerus
    as a feathered spider
        runs behind the shadow
in my brain
        while the voices in the drums
cry in old emblems.

    Dr Death drafts
        my oppression bills
for his crystal estate
        under the lapping
of sands.

    Then comes my highly prized
        lover, crested
in doors of stone.

THERE YOU GO BABY.

Agony under agony
it's making me
burn-up
I wish I could
hang-up somewhere;
I turn
minutes into hours
and life's a drag
without
this kind of thing
and everything
is so unhappy
really
I can't fall in love
because
it's a natural killer.

I dream & dream
of Harlequin
and I am having one
of those sexless nights
where birds fly out
of the mouth
with their tails
on fire.

I think of Harlequin
I think;
he's about three
streets long
with a burning black
bush above his mouth

and he's so beautifully minded
he could be god
to me right now
if only he could just
hold one of these pains
it would be such a help;
I must like
giving-up
because
I've noticed him
walk by me
like a bubble.

I AM FROZEN WITH KNOWLEDGE.

Sleep in my eyes if you want a home
but don't talk
sounds smoke me out
and I bar all time from washing.

I am of age and I see
the morning through a body.

Wishes turn into eyes
& my lover burns by me;
our kingdom is life
& governments dry out our thoughts
like a storm is fur
as we buckle the shells of wisdom
our feet kick shadows into colours
but we string the seasons together.

The gypsy in me is gassed to death
but still desires a golden frame
and the longhair on the universe
grows down to my shoulders.

I expect the painter is beyond
my greatest thought;
the colours he gives for war.

I watch him fall into corners
where razor blades
becomes his nearest friend;
my painter shows a real knowledge
and takes little from the mind.

In all his maps there's fear.

The face of music is out
but perhaps just lost down space
like water under the sea.

I finger the dreams
there's bad weather;
no free fearing
but I lay in my own bones

"IN THIS SLAUGHTER-HOUSE"

In this slaughter-house
intellect
moves as a dance
& a spell of sleep
wouldn't do it any harm;
But the established-folk
want the last secret-seed
in the brain cells
only to enjoy the history
of wit.

I am a frightened animal
I trust in nothing
& suffer the penalty;
I wish to go
instead of being stripped
by each new genius.

Identical to a worm
I run on a nerve
with the dread
of being eaten alive
yet humans want
to soil the mind
on a banquet.

I am an imbecile
drugged out of this world
because I run.

I am exhausted
from trying to close these eyes
in wandering
through memories & myths;
I must hide
& die.

"THE EARTH MOVES ON CRACKED MIRRORS"

the earth moves on cracked mirrors

I got a crowbar for the crows

simple complexion   salts the mind / big fuss

HE IS A ROSE.

If I were to put it that we are two flowers,
then he is the rose
because he holds the thorns.
I know
he knows
we are not good for one another.
He casts the stones
and I
throw the darkness.
The pair of us
have a falling pain upon each other's burns
our eyes never meet
our words never ring.
I have the last thought
he
dear he, has the last word.

AGE.

For Cressida

I'm sex in a body
and no I but no eye sees
                              I love
In me there's not a pin of guilt
Nor a hair of religion
and only I, blood of me
will fire.

The mirror shows all an idiot
and that is where I exist;
Dreams fool
and life fancies itself
is this vulgarity
Life?

I had a great design on flesh
(some one studied the Gods
for his own secrets) but
Now
                              time
lets me die around myself.

17-10-64

TO A ROMANTIC (ROBIN).

The slender day trembles, without love
like a sleeping flower
far from the veins of habit
that blow a cutting pain
beneath the sheets of night.
Fresh as flowers
kisses drop into the mind of his heart.
And his true mind had a ticket for a trip
down a valley covered in heather.
The graceful light shines on satisfaction,
or a desolated body in the autumn –
of a dark room.
The anger of blackness fires between
the towers of flesh,
as only one body is permitted to vomit
to spread love and sorrow –
among the stars.
Lost,
lost is this day.

OUR FRIENDSHIP BEGAN ON THE FOUNDATIONS OF BUILDING A BASEMENT.

For J.H. Lindsay

Summer.
With all its hot days —
under a desire I work.
And not for the waste of life
nor to laugh at the world.
But to kill a pain
which eats through my heart.

Digging the clay
with the power I have —
in these arms of mine.
The more the spade digs
the harder the work becomes.

"ALAS, I HAVE CORRUPTED BEAUTY"

Alas, I have corrupted beauty
I rise to the morning
To find I've slept with my enemy
And now I see the world is hollow
For I am a chip in his heart
Bleeding the wood, which was once strong
I look at Every-Body
And flesh becomes a sun, and my blindness
I care for flesh, blood & kisses
Then like a cat —
I dream at every eye

THE BAYSWATER BOY.

(you're looking queer, today)

I run around in a flat circle
And the dust inside me
Looks boyish
But has no bone, and is still a virgin
I try to remember life
Love or death
And a soft had fur face of her
But it's absolutely shamed
Is it the laughing day?
O, Oh please ease the ice in me,
For I am playing a game with life
I am a cowboy
Out to get the man that hurt me,
The old crying pain is silent
And yet it echoes,
And it's reason is vacant
The clear consciousness of its emotions
Brings the attention and the small degree of hope
I said to myself feeling petty for life
"I illustrate nothing by living"
And the agony is not the study of religion.
I sacrifice my ideas for the love of my friends
And the purpose of life
Shows on my face
For pain is a dictionary of people
O to be a stone
And sudden death

THE WASTE.

I knew a grave-yard in my childhood
Where the highest winds blew.
It was cold for the heart,
There were no honey gates
To let in joy.
No mother
With arms to hold my heart.
But thought took its course
And turned into wisdom
And this body moves slower and slower
Into infinity.

This mouth decays like an old house
They are but words to you, friend,
They are neither hotted-up by desires
Nor by the sweet bitterness of your wounds,
Only time has given me clear sight.
My head is dull now
For nothing flows in
Because nothing flows out,
For my mind has begun to melt rocks
And every day is Ash-day.
And who should know better than you
That the content of this body
Is a good portrait of the dead.

I look, and I don't think.
But I can hang God
On a line of words.
So damp, dirty and cold is this body
That the waste looks like pleasure.

Time passes
Whilst the roots of lilac
Grow into the heart,
Until there are no senses.
Lilac is for people,
Good, silent people
Trapped in deep wooden boxes.

THE END OF THIS DAY.

So the darling blackness of day
calls my tiredness,
Even the echo of the voice is tired
and the hours note my aching bones
restless,
like the sea, I seem to lie on a bed of rocks.
My mind is moving in simpleness,
for happiness,
a few fingernails run up and down the flesh
until it hurts
and all my cigarettes have gone to smoke or ash.
At night these two eyes are colourless
and they bleed water
yes, these eyes
in the starborn night shed of summer tears
for my Love,
and I know
tomorrow will be bright
and I will look with the same eyes
for new things
and the same happiness as yesterday.
Slowly
this world is fading out of existence
fluttering in a few thoughts
burning unsteadily to nothing, soon all will be gone
the hard and flowery language of sound
will die in my darkness
and my own body will become a piece of steel
my prayers will also disappear
but I bless the one that awakes me tomorrow
for renewing my life.

THE BOY.

what gentry has the boy to play
but the inside of his pants
the plant of love grows
and mothers made and children know
his heart will bottle all pain
and two gods
will field and hang their hocks
whilst lady love
will be but a whisper through a straw
the wind shall be his lamb
and silences a mother
and his cream, the break of her scream
his bed any bed
will make an eternal battlefield of response

the young boy
stands in the warmth of desires
adam left his print in him
awake and hunt me, you savage
before I burn up my desire
you for me
can make time
this object will not fly through thought

mother
why was I not mother
to you
to your sucking bone
the world is a walking gentleman
and will not share this bed
god without a face
holds a respect

but I have no answer for myself
the quietness of your childish heart
eyes my body
and will loiter in my image.

AFTER LAST NIGHT SHE SAID.

The man I kissed
was not god,
and it was not the devil
in my desire,
but the encouragement
to live
she said.

LOOKING BACK.

On this world, passing
turning and touching friends,
it is courage that makes us people
and the shadows that make
our weakness weak.
At the noise of some poor soul in pain
we sometimes laugh,
and die in a pool of dead weeds.
A glancing look at another's limbs
makes us mad in the race for love.
Our knowledge never explores,
but rumbles on in darkness.
The tender flesh we held at birth
gave us choice, only to provide us with
snow-white swans and thoughts
we never could resist.
We love
for the chance to touch flesh
and move blood,
to embrace the present whilst
covering the future with our hands.

DREAM OF YOU.

You lifted your head
and quivered like a rose
searching for thought,
then stopped
when you reached beauty.
The movement was clean
and fast
like a flame;
Your realisation
burnt a smile across your face.
The thought was involving no one.

The burial
brought yourself to yourself
then you were peaceful
and fell into weariness
of your true age.
And I loved you
as if I turned my head in dreams
for lost sunsets.

LOVE AND HATE.

love theme
moves like a symphony
with the tenderness
like an orange or golden
september
during each sunset
much joy and sorrow
is lost
my belief
at each sudden death
of every day
there is a chariot
full of sweet roses
and the scent of the roses
falls on the loved
the loving and the lover
as it rides through
blue skies

hate is sordid
just like wet dust
hate
moves like a fountain
it keeps coming up
then over
hate moves like love
it moves together
until it kills
the thing it most needs,
hate comes from way back
from childhood.

EDITORIAL NOTES.

During his lifetime, Mark Hyatt published around 40 poems in little magazines. His most prominent appearance was in the anthology *Children of Albion: Poetry of the Underground in Britain* (1969); his most obscure was probably a year later, in *Lift*, the mimeo magazine of the Barnoldswick Congregational Church, whose editor was a teenager.

Hyatt's is a heavily mediated and complex body of work. After his death, some of his poems were published in three chapbooks, and around 75 further poems appeared in mimeo magazines, independent journals, and anthologies. His poems were edited according to various principles, and were sometimes retitled, excerpted, or otherwise re-arranged. These publications were often based on second-hand transcriptions.

This edition draws on four sources: 1) the poems Hyatt published during his lifetime in little magazines; 2) poems published posthumously, including the three chapbooks: *How Odd* (1973), *Eleven Poems* (1974), and *A Different Mercy* (1976); 3) a private collection of papers belonging to Lucy and Mick O'Shea; 4) xeroxes of Hyatt's work in the archive of J.H. Prynne now held at the University Library, Cambridge. The latter forms the core of this book, and has been the reference point for our editorial decisions. Prynne preserved the order and arrangement of the material very carefully, which provided a skeleton of the dates of composition on which to build. We choose to present the poems in reverse-chronological order, starting in the early 1970s and working backwards.

Our sequencing is guided by Hyatt's own organisation of his poems into folders and envelopes, often with working titles (e.g., *Too Good To Be True*, or *Harlequin of the North*). These clusters, replicated diligently in the Prynne xeroxes, provide important evidence of the work Hyatt wanted to retain, as well as his process of drafting and revisiting his own work (some

poems are included in several folders and notebooks). Over-
leaf, we've included a table of contents for the xeroxes, which
provides important information about the work Hyatt wished
to retain. This includes sequencings for unrealised publica-
tions along with more haphazard arrangements, both of which
have influenced the architecture of this book.

Of the 136 poems we print here, 48 are – to the best of
our knowledge – previously unpublished in any form. Among
the remainder, only 15 of our selection were published during
Hyatt's lifetime. 45 of the poems exist in more than one man-
uscript state.

Hyatt's delayed literacy meant that he often sought help
in preparing his poems for publication. Mark's lovers and
friends – particularly Cressida Lindsay, Donald "Atom"
Haworth, and Lucy O'Shea – corrected his poems at his
request. For Hyatt, the intimacy of a poem's making and cir-
culation wasn't a neutral fact, and the struggle for articulation
goes to the core of his poetics.

The archive preserves these traces, both literal and
implicit, in a way that this edition can't wholly represent. We
have made our decisions on a poem-by-poem basis, compar-
ing extant manuscript copies with published versions (where
such versions exist), and establishing a preferred source in
each case. We tend, where no evidence of contact between
Hyatt and the publisher exists, to prefer versions in Hyatt's
possession. We have taken note of handwritten alterations
and prior editorial interventions, and have exercised our own
judgement. This process is indicated in detail in the follow-
ing notes. We have followed Mark's distinct style of titling his
poems with a definitive period.

Unless indicated otherwise, the text of *So Much for
Life* follows what the editors understand to be Hyatt's own
latest draft or final fair copy, prepared for circulation or
posterity. Xeroxed typewritten (tw) and holographic (hg)
– i.e., handwritten – manuscripts in J.H. Prynne's archive
comprise the primary text. Seven poems are drawn from
the O'Shea papers, either because no extant copy exists in

the Prynne archive, or because the O'Shea version aligns closely with an instance published during Hyatt's lifetime. We have tried to avoid legitimising Hyatt's work by cleaning it up or 'improving' it, subjecting it to standardisation, but at the same time, we have tried to avoid fetishizing errors and slips, the stigmata of authenticity. We have tended to preserve moments of grammatical ambiguity or even confusion, and have preserved the idiosyncrasies of Hyatt's writing practice, those 'errors' we see as creative and productive.

The information in [square brackets] refers to the location of the preferred source within Prynne's sequentially numbered xeroxes. Information in (curved brackets) notes the location of other extant drafts in the xeroxes or in the O'Shea collection. Titles are given as an approximation of their appearance in manuscript form (all caps, lowercase, etc). Previous publications are given in chronological order, and have been consulted in all cases.

Hyatt's capitalisation of words, especially in handwritten material, is erratic. We've interpreted this on a poem-by-poem basis, rather than making an attempt to standardize. We routinely emend obvious mis-typings and spelling mistakes, but only rarely adjust punctuation. The exception to this is apostrophes, which we have regularised. Corrections to obvious misspelling, emendations of capitalization, and minor punctuation have, as a rule, been made silently.

The following notes record significant and/or problematic differences between manuscript and publications; record variants in intermediate drafts; and flag editorial alterations. Hyatt's typewritten manuscripts often include handwritten emendations, particularly at the intermediate draft stage. We have described substantial instances as far as possible, and have noted where we depart from these suggestions and revisions. No notes or comments on the manuscript status indicate that the source text is fair copy.

The following schematic is based on the Inventory of Mark Hyatt Manuscripts in the archive of J.H. Prynne. It gives an overview of the xeroxes, and uses the sequential numbering we refer to in the notes. Our running order for *So Much For Life* is based on these clusters, interleaved with runs of his published poems from the chapbooks *How Odd* and *Eleven Poems* and the anthology *Children of Albion*. The transition between 'Pre-Leeds' and 'Post-Leeds' happens somewhere around the poem Sh *Everyboy*.

I. "POST-LEEDS"

A. LOOSE SHEETS (3-212)
B. FOLDERS, BOOKS, SEPARATE BATCHES

    i. "Fair Copies" (215-224)
    ii. "Manuscripts" (226-237)
    iii. Notebook (Last Poems) (239-250)
    iv. Notebook "Not to be looked at, understood?" (253-263)
    v. Black foolscap notebook (i) (267-331)
    vi. Black foolscap notebook (ii) Marked "?" (337-372)
    vii. Green Folder (377-412)
    viii. Brown paper bag (414-431)
    ix. Blue folder marked "KLEE'S FEARS" (433-525)
    x. Blue folder marked "April" (527-563)
    xi. Blue folder marked "Too Good to be True" (576-631)

II. "PRE-LEEDS"

    i. "Loose papers" (634-678)
    ii. Typed poems in blue folder marked "Early" (680-762)
    iii. Typed play (764-786)
    iv. Mostly typed sheets in an envelope (788-891)
    v. Mostly typed sheets in beige folder marked "Roses & Fire" (894-1085)
    vi. Mostly typed sheets in an envelope marked "The Cherry & The Bumble Bee An Anthology of Poems by Mark Hyatt" ("very early texts") (1088-1356)
    vii. Sheets in an envelope marked "Poems from Paris and Other" ("very early texts") (1358-1528)
    viii. Blue folder ("mostly fragments") (1530-1582)

ADDITIONAL

    i. Red foolscap manuscript book "Harlequin from the North and Other Poems" (1583-1606)
    ii. Loose papers (1607-1609)

O Poem.
[3 tw] (882 tw)
New Departures 7/8 and 10/11
[Double Issue] (1975).

Poor Soul
[4 tw] (112 tw)
Previously unpublished.
112 includes handwritten emenda-
tions (apostrophes, capitalization)
and suggested line-breaks. 112
variants and emendations include
'bloody lonely' in l.2, deleted by
hand; 'and' opening lines 5, 11, 12,
15, 22, deleted by hand; addition of
dashes, replaced by semi colons in 4
(l.11-12); addition of a period (l.4).
Present text changes l.5 'wanta' to
'want a'.

Yes!
[6 tw] (327 hg)
Global Tapestry Journal 3 (1972).
327 includes period at the end of
l.14.

Puberty of Puck.
[7 tw] (10 tw; 528 tw)
A Different Mercy (1976); *Sal
Mimeo* 13 (2013).
Present text follows 528 in print-
ing 'no longer' in l.25, where 7, 10,
and *ADM* present the compound
'nolonger.' Foot of 10 includes
typed 'Love Atom' and handwrit-
ten 'love / Mark Hyatt . xxx'. 528
emends by hand, deleting 'how-
ever' at start of l.18 and clarifying
concluding three words as 'any
wild space'.

Hashish on Sunday
[8-9 tw]
Previously unpublished.
Handwritten emendations capital-
izing l.1 and correcting penultimate
line 'cude' to 'crude.' Present text
changes l.21 '11-hours' to '11-hour'.

"Spirit of who's outside"
[17 hg]
Previously unpublished.
Untitled, though a note on the top
right reads 'got it'.

half bread
[30 ts]
Previously unpublished.
In 30 the final word at l.13 is ambig-
uous due to overtyping. Present text
prints 'puck'; 'punch' is also plausi-
ble. Present text changes title from
'half bread'; changes l.1 'Imhalf' to
'I'm half'; changes l.8 'ignorants as'
to 'ignorance has'.

come into the world
[31 tw]
Equofinality 2 (1984).
Equofinality prints 'I miss those
friends' in l.1.

"it's all sighs"
[32 tw]
Previously unpublished.
Present text changes l.5 and l.6,
'indifferents' to 'indifference'.

Delicate
[36 tw] (428-9 hg)
The Literary Supplement 20 (August
1974); *A Different Mercy* (1976).
Handwritten emendation to 36
adds colon or semi colon to l.3
(present text prints colon); ques-
tion mark added by hand to l.6,
retained in present text. 428-9 is
only faintly legible.

Individual
[37 tw] (198 hg)
Collection 7 (Autumn 1970);
Equofinality 2 (1984); *Not Love
Alone: A Modern Gay Anthology*
(1985).
Handwritten emendation to 37
alters 'case' to 'chase'.

Pretty Common
[45 tw]
Earth Ship 7 (December 1971/
January 1972).
Handwritten emendations to 45
including l.6 'on' to 'over'; l.11
'around' to 'round'; l.13 separation
of 'nolonger' by backslash; l.16
'make them' proposed change to
'made to' (followed in present text);
l.17 'how' inserted before 'ugly'.
45 is untitled but printed as 'Pretty
Common' *Earth Ship*, with title
likely supplied by Hyatt.

It's all in the past now
[46 tw]
Earth Ship 7 (December 1971/
January 1972).
Handwritten emendations to 46
including to spelling, capital-
ization, and punctuation; note
proposes 'trying' to replace 'so he
tires', adopted in present text; l.9
includes handwritten annotation
'word missed out', with suggestions
for line-ending, including 'flare',
'gleam', 'glare', 'flicker': present
text prints 'glare'.

**"It's deep inside, this
nothingness"**
[49 tw]
A Different Mercy (1976).
49 is untitled. Handwritten emen-
dation adds comma after 'inside'
and proposes with question mark
insertion of 'the' into l.2, 'most
of time', which *A Different Mercy*
follows, printing 'most of the time':
present text retains 'most of time' as
preference.

looking for a poem
[51 tw]
Previously unpublished.
Present text changes l.1 'Almost a
sleep' to 'Almost asleep'.

between you and humanity
[53 tw]
Greedy Shark (1973).
Some significant variant readings
between 53 and *Greedy Shark*: l.3
reads 'Sometime' (present text
follows handwritten emendation to
'Some time' with backslash); l.14,
Greedy Shark gives 'sons of the soil';
l.36 reads 'and that's been going up
and down the country hills'. Present
text follows 53. Typescript has
frequent handwritten emendations
to spelling, punctuation (notably full
stops lines 2, 4, 6, 8, 9, 22, 25, 29, 37,
38, 41, 42), and capitalization; addi-
tion of 'a' in l.1, l.42; change of 'then'
to 'to' in l.33; 'A gave' to 'I give' l.5;
insertion of 'But' in l.14; deletion of
'luck' at end of l.21; capitalization
of 'dale' in l.31; addition of comma
after 'My son' in last line. Present
text hyphenates 'slower-witted', and
changes 'maybe' in l.26 to 'may be'.

hello
[54 tw]
Greedy Shark (1973).
Greedy Shark lineates the poem to
the left margin. Lineation in 54 is
slightly wayward, likely as a result
of the typewriter rather than intent;
present text follows lineation as
closely as possible. Variant reading
of l.30 in *Greedy Shark*: 'of ours,
some time back'.

new brave wired ones
[55 tw]
Global Tapestry Journal 4
(February 1973).
Publication in *Global Tapestry Journal*
capitalizes all lines and gives vari-
ant reading of l.21: 'we are so clean
together'. Handwritten emendations
to 55 including some spellings, and
include 'going' for 'go' in l.2 (followed
in present text); suggested change of

'we go to tell' to 'we are going to tell' in l.3 (not followed in present text); insertion of 'could' in l.4 to read 'clean you could eat' (not followed in present text); insertion of question mark at the end of l.6 (followed in present text); 'are' inserted in l.8 (followed in present text). Possible comma in l.12 after 'so far', not followed in present text; comma suggested in l.13 after 'so-clean', followed in present text.

"Hark! the dearie mark"
[72 tw]
Human Handkerchief 3 (Summer 1974).
72 gives 'champaign champaign camp' at l.7. Present text follows the publication in *Human Handkerchief*, and gives 'Champagne champagne camp'. *Human Handkerchief* presents minor variants in punctuation.

OUT OF SPITE
[75 tw] (531 tw)
Previously unpublished.

"the jade thieves carve the wind"
[81 tw]
Turpin Double Issue 7/8 (February 1974); *A Different Mercy* (1976).

the sun sweats salt
[100 tw]
Previously unpublished.
Handwritten emendations to 100 including capitalization and punctuation; addition of comma at the end of l.1 not followed in present text.

Green Life
[116 tw]
A Different Mercy (1976); *Equofinality* 2 (1984).

Poem
[O'Shea] [120 hg]

Previously unpublished.
120 all in capitals. Present text follows the O'Shea version, giving the title 'Poem'.

"bring back youth robbers"
[121 tw] (215 tw)
Partial publication in *Poetry Review* 65.2/3 (1975).
Present text follows 121, previously unpublished in this state. The ten lines from 'hunting key holes for pity' to 'we are into shit arse and soul' are circled by hand: they appear extracted at 215, and are printed in *Poetry Review* 65.2/3 (1975). In 121 l.3 reads 'spead like a cat', suggesting 'speed' or 'spread', or perhaps even 'spayed': present text prints 'spread'. Present text incorporates an additional comma from 215 in l.26 after 'you'.

"cry baby cry"
[136 tw]
Previously unpublished.
136 l.13 ambiguous as overtyping suggests either 'in' or 'on'. Present text alters l.12 'rooks' to 'rocks'.

queers
[144 hg]
Previously unpublished.
Line after poem with note underneath: 'Last words are never / famous only sick!'

"The Moth is back, just peeled out of the skin"
[153 tw]
A Different Mercy (1976).
Present text follows 153 and *ADM* in retaining a terminal comma.

separate noises
[168 tw]
Previously unpublished.
Handwritten emendation to 168

adds 'THINKS' to l.8, followed in present text.

"All I want is courage"
[170 hg]
Previously unpublished.

"white angels move in the wind"
[171 tw]
A Different Mercy (1976); *Poets on Writing* (1992).

life is a shock
[174 tw]
Previously unpublished.

"I can't sell my penis because"
[180 tw]
Previously unpublished.
Modest handwritten emendations to 180 including capitalization; change of 'I got' to 'I've got' in l.4 followed in present text; 'THE' and 'NIBBLE' inserted into l.16, followed in present text; 'I've' inserted into l.17, accepted in present text; in l.15 'right' is crossed out (retained in present text as preference).

HYDE PARK
[182 hg]
Skylight 2 (Winter-Spring 1972). Holograph in all capitals. *Skylight* gives full stop at end of l.1.

How Odd
(316-21 hg) [189-92 tw]
How Odd (1973).
Present text follows *How Odd* with some variants. *How Odd* has 'These' at stanza 7, l.1, where 189-92 and 316-21 have 'There'. Present text incorporates a variant from 316-21 at stanza 3, l.4, adding 'thin' to 'and thin children hot with jazz'. The holograph version, 316-21, includes two stanzas after stanza 18 ('Local people...') reading:

O.K. I enjoy sex, tiny silences
of not knowing what sense come next,
love, breast kisses harbouring in my eyes
you leave lanterns in the blood

naked I am no-where a hero,
but like a whore I love creation
my arse is a comedy in the streets
and glitter for our touches

316-21 also includes three stanzas (the middle one cancelled) after stanza 19 ('Name me...'), reading:

to see if your world is my world,
and try not to look like the image of
                                    splendour
I won't prostitute dead lies for pleasure
but I need a door bolt to keep me in.

I will lick your shit up if you lick mine
and give no more than we want
I am ~~even a penis lover~~
I am for us, you, everybody and I

soon through the streets community
people will smudge into each other's dance
and sing like sirens from hell,
then I will realize I am in.

Taken
[185 hg] (O'Shea tw)
How Odd (1973).
Present text follows *How Odd*. In 185, l.3 has 'illiterate', amended to 'illustrate' in marginal annotation. Version in O'Shea Papers is near identical, except it prints 'f---, what a mess I live in!' at l.12, where *How Odd* prints 'fuck'. In O'Shea the line also appears, cancelled, between l.10 and l.11.

Border Line
[193 tw] (311 hg; O'Shea tw)
How Odd (1973); *New Departures* 7/8 and 10/11 [Double Issue] (1975).
O'Shea Papers version is without a stanza break, and is typed beneath a letter to Mick O'Shea from Belthorn dated '15-12-70'. A note follows the final line of the poem: '—salesman

just knocked trying to sell me broom and brush, ha i let the dust & dirt stay where god put's it, I no women even at the best of times,—'. At the foot of the page appears 'when cornflakes fart', titled 'Poem'.

poor sod

[186 hg] (194 ts; O'Shea tw)
How Odd (1973).
Present text follows *How Odd*. In the O'Shea Papers, the typescript page includes the poem 'Taken.'

Puffed-Out

[127 tw]
How Odd (1973).
127 l.4 reads 'headpains'; typewritten change of 'even' to 'ever' in l.4; handwritten emendation deleting 'of' in l.5 ('half of the'), followed in present text.

"Trying to remember what memory"

[118 tw] (310 hg)
How Odd (1973).
Both 118 and 310 punctuate l.7 'shaking life; frightened': present text follows *How Odd* in printing 'shaking life, frightened'.

A DEFINITE CHOICE

[271 hg]
How Odd (1973).
Present text follows *How Odd* and 271, including capitalization. 271 includes poem beginning 'soft head'.

Work and Wonder

[114 tw] (122 tw)
How Odd (1973).
Present text follows *How Odd* and 114. 114 is fair copy except the final line, where 'I' is deleted from 'evenings I be intimate'. 122 is an earlier draft, giving handwritten title WORK AND WONDER, and handwritten emendations

throughout. 122 gives variant reading of l.13: 'and embracingly I wonder', and includes an additional line after l.25, reading, 'and I quiver social living prices'. Opening line inserts 'at' into 'work my job'; final line reads 'evenings I am intimate', 'I am' replaced by 'BE'; l.25 and l.26 begin 'and', both deleted. l.16 changes 'image' to 'Imagine'; l.20 reads 'I have very few feeding as a man' with handwritten emendation 'I HAVE VERY FEW OF THE FEELINGS OF A MAN'.

HOME-WALK

[226 hg]
Published as 'Homewalk' in *Lift* (c. 1970).
Present text follows the punctuation of 226.

THIS POEM

[211-12 tw] (O'Shea tw)
Collection 7 (Autumn 1970).
Version in O'Shea Papers is addressed 121 Belthorn Rd, Blackburn, and includes a note: 'This is going through my head'. 211-2 includes line numbers (5, 10, 15…). Handwritten emendation of 'error' to 'era' in l.10; 'weep' to 'act' in l.31; 'nobody' to 'nothing' in l.56.

"Withdrawals on demand"

[217 tw]
Previously unpublished.
217 capitalizes l.1; l.4 emended by hand to include parentheses; ambiguity around line-break between l.5 and l.6: typed break is at 'simplicity', but handwritten emendation inserts the earlier enjambment, retained in present text.

deep silence

[315 hg]
The Literary Supplement 20 (August

1974); *A Different Mercy* (1976).
In 315, l.5 reads 'a man that's has
tattooed'; *The Literary Supplement*
gives variant, reading 'a man that
has tattooed'. Present text follows *A
Different Mercy*, which gives 'a man
has tattooed'.

"just woke up to a lot of light"
[298 hg]
A Different Mercy (1976).

A DREAM
[299 hg]
Equofinality 2 (1984).

IS IT NOW
[323 hg]
A Different Mercy (1976).

MAN by AGE
[328 hg]
Previously unpublished.

"soon the mind will be heavy"
[329 hg]
A Different Mercy (1976).
329 gives 'experiences flutters' in l.6.
Present text follows *A Different Mercy*
in the variant 'experiences flutter'.

growing peas
[344 hg]
Poetry Review 65.2/3 (1975); *Global
Tapestry Journal* 8 (September
1979); *Palantir* 15 (July 1980).
344 has 'listen to aeroplane engines'.
Present text follows *Global Tapestry
Journal* in variant 'listening to aero-
plane engines'.

A Shiner
[346 hg]
A Different Mercy (1976).
Present text follows *A Different
Mercy*. 346 has 'how' for 'our' in
l.14 and penultimate line.

I tell you now
[348 hg]
Previously unpublished.
348 l.21 reads 'your gone to fine
charm ain't worth shit', altered in
present text to 'you're going to find
charm ain't worth shit'.

SADDAY
[368 hg]
Strange Faeces, No. 8 (1972);
Grosseteste *Review* 7.1-3
(Summer 1974).
Strange Faeces prints the title as
'SADDAY' and lineates; *Grosseteste
Review* prints 'SAD DAY' as a
prose-poem, and with variant
'moonlit' for 'moonhit' in l.2.
Present text follows 368 and pub-
lication in *Strange Faeces* with title
adjusted to 'Sad Day'.

FROM HOSPITAL
[244 hg]
Previously unpublished.
Punctuation as in 244: 'sucks 'n
kisses, smokes n' jokes'. Present text
is taken from a notebook used in
hospital, marked in the inventory as
'(Last Poems)'.

'that's it really, nothing too big under wind'
[260 hg]
The Literary Supplement 20 (August
1974).
Present text is taken from a note-
book used in hospital, marked in the
inventory as '(Last Poems)'.

Dice
[229 hg]
Eleven Poems (1974); *Global Tapestry
Journal* 8 (September 1979).
229 gives no capital in l.4. Present
text follows *Eleven Poems* in
capitalization.

Bootless
[233 tw] (393 tw)
Eleven Poems (1974).

Mug's Game
[218 tw] (235 tw; 391 tw; 610 tw)
Eleven Poems (1974).
391 includes a comma at the end of
l.5 and capitalizes l.6.

Rattling Focus Where Do You Go
[228 tw]
Eleven Poems (1974).
Handwritten emendations to
228 including punctuation and
capitalization.

The Composer's Fingers
[234 tw] (388 tw; 611 tw; 612 tw)
Eleven Poems (1974).

Daggers.
[219 tw] (231 tw)
Eleven Poems (1974).
Handwritten emendations to 231
including capitalization; addition of
commas to read 'Sleep, if I could,'
in l.1; addition of em-dashes at the
end of lines 3, 6, 9, 13: all followed
in present text.

Schizoid
[222 tw] (236 tw; 607 tw; 622 tw)
Eleven Poems (1974).

Tame
[103 tw] (221 tw; 232 tw; 386 tw)
Eleven Poems (1974).

A Regular Guy
[34 tw]
Eleven Poems (1974); *Global Tapestry
Journal* 8 (September 1979).
Present text follows 34 on which the
title is handwritten. *Eleven Poems*
gives variant readings: l.15, 'I went,
like in a party, so'; l.16, 'evil was I'.

Wine
[220 tw]
Eleven Poems (1974); *A Different
Mercy* (1976); *Global Tapestry
Journal* 8 (September 1979).
A Different Mercy prints without title.

INCONCLUSIVE ENGAGEMENT
[230 tw]
Eleven Poems (1974); *Global Tapestry
Journal* 8 (September 1979).
230 includes handwritten title;
'machine gun' is altered to 'shot-
gun'; addition of line 'A BROKEN
SKELETON, A BIRD SINGS –'
at l.21.

"Two queers live on a hill"
[377 hg]
A Different Mercy (1976).
Present text follows *A Different
Mercy*: in 377, l.4 reads 'quite' rather
than 'quiet'.

"love in the shadow of summer"
[379 hg]
A Different Mercy (1976).
Both 379 and *A Different Mercy*
read: 'Also I got drain my penis of
life' at l. 18. Present text alters to
'Also I got to drain my penis of life.'

POEM
[392 tw] (417 tw; 490 hg; 613 tw)
A Different Mercy (1976).
490 cancels 'human' and replaces
with 'man' in last line.

so so
[406 tw]
A Different Mercy (1976);
Equofinality 2 (1984).
Present text follows 406 and
Equofinality in printing 'then' at the
end of l.5: *A Different Mercy* gives vari-
ant reading 'them'. Present text follows
406 in giving a terminal full-stop.

OF SOMETHING ELSE
[418 tw]
Turpin Double Issue 7/8 (February 1974).
Handwritten title in 418, which includes emendations to capitalization, punctuation, and end of l.7 changing 'which' to 'that'.

Dazzle: Lament Diagram
[423 tw]
A Different Mercy (1976).
A Different Mercy gives variant reading of 'frightening' for 'frighting' at l.4. Present text follows 423.

POEM
[425 tw]
Previously unpublished.

The Day's Sage/'The eternal day breaks out'
[434 tw]
Lift (c. 1970); *A Different Mercy* (1976).
Lineation of 434 is ambiguous between left aligned and something more various (as in printing in *A Different Mercy*). 434 includes handwritten emendations to capitalization and minor corrections. 434 has no title but the poem is published in *Lift* as 'The Day's Sage', taken from the poem's last seven lines, bracketed by hand and excised in 434, which read:

then the immortal sun of all skies
soaring the heat of the soul's heart
burning down through the day sage
light heat streaming pleasure beyond
    heaven
cushioning the ground in sobs
this sun is buttercup sweet to the mountains
and scents blend thinking in paint

"from the poor freak streets comes a lad"
[440 tw]
A Different Mercy (1976).

Present text proposes the variant 'slowly' for 'slow' in l.10. There remains ambiguity around 'quirt' in l.13, which might read 'quid' for payment or 'quart' for liquor. We retain 'quirt' with reference to the dictionary: 'A whip; *spec.* a riding whip with a short handle and a braided leather lash.'

JACK'S UNION
[442 hg]
Previously unpublished.
Variations in capitalization suggest regularizing to either majority capitals or lowercase, present text adopting the latter.

"i have drunken the bromide"
[468 tw]
A Different Mercy (1976).

"Let him go in mind"
[473 tw]
Previously unpublished.
473 includes handwritten emendations to capitalization and punctuation. Present text follows holograph emendation of final line, switching word order and adding punctuation. The typed text reads: 'ain't marvellous great lovers boys'. The lineation of 473 is various, but suggests incidental typewriter misalignment rather than deliberate composition.

"oral pictures of love"
[477 tw]
Previously unpublished.
Present text maintains small spacing in l.24 and 29 which appear to be deliberate.

Break My Name.
[387 tw] (489 hg; 603 tw)
Previously unpublished.

489 lacks commas. l.10 reads 'I thinking of his thinking'. Handwritten changes to 603 add 'an' to l.6; 'and' to l.10; 'And I' is crossed out at the start of l.11.

"hey golden limbs"
[499 tw]
Previously unpublished.

moon tune
[507 tw]
Previously unpublished.

nothing to do but love you
[508 tw]
Previously unpublished.

"a high height when thinking"
[518 tw]
A Different Mercy (1976).

COUNTRY POEM.
[421 tw] (520 hg)
A Different Mercy (1976).

high blues
[522 tw]
A Different Mercy (1976).
522 has handwritten emendations to the opening typewritten lines, inserting the full stop at the end of l.1, changing 'its' to 'it's', in l.2, and significantly altering 'who I balance' to 'how I balance'. *A Different Mercy* prints: 'yes to you and no. / It's terrible how I balance': present text follows *A Different Mercy* but retains lowercase 'it's'.

"Now I live in the north country"
[525 tw]
A Different Mercy (1976).
525 features brackets inserted by hand in l.16, reading, 'I have told you now (he has told me so)'; also in l.18, reading, 'it is not (in not) in him to reveal': present text follows

A Different Mercy, which interprets these brackets as editorial excisions.

K.Y. Poem
[532 hg] (47 hg; 577 hg)
Previously unpublished.
Variations in capitalization across 47, 532 and 577; 47 capitalizes line openings and includes a comma at the end of l.4; 577 capitalizes line openings and includes a semi-colon at the end of l.4: present text follows 532.

True Homosexual Love.
[580 tw]
The Curiously Strong: Final Issue IV.9 & 10 (1975); *Equofinality* 2 (1984).

Dear Friend Go Away, Please.
[581 tw]
Previously unpublished.

Nerves Blotted Out
(227 ts) [583 tw]
The Literary Supplement 20 (August 1974); *Equofinality* 2 (1984); *Not Love Alone: A Modern Gay Anthology* (1985).
All published versions give variant reading 'skillful' in stanza 5, l.2: present text follows 227 and 583 in printing 'skullful'.

"this is a terrible bit of writing"
[585 tw]
Previously unpublished.

EXTENDED MOVEMENT.
[416 tw] (601 tw; 609 tw)
A Different Mercy (1976); *Poets on Writing: 1979-1991* (1992).
601 includes minor handwritten emendations. 609 includes minor handwritten changes around spacing and capitalization: stanza 4, l.2 has 'like' crossed out before 'emergency'; stanza 5 l.1 changes the final

phrase from 'life seasoning brilliant' to 'life's brilliant seasons'.

So Much For Life

Pause 2 (Winter 1969/Spring 1970); *Equofinality* 2 (1984).
No known manuscript. *Equofinality* reprints from *Pause*.

"I love my arse to be sucked"

[624 tw]
Previously unpublished.
The layout of present text follows 624.

between chaos I come

[625 tw]
The Literary Supplement 20 (August 1974).
Handwritten emendations to 625 including capitalization and one instance of spelling.

"desert bones"

[627 tw]
Grosseteste Review 7.1-3 (Summer 1974).
627 is in a complicated state, due to attempts to squeeze the last lines in at the bottom of the page, along with typewritten additions and a handwritten clarification. *Grosseteste Review* offers variant punctuation throughout, including redaction of line end dashes on l.11 and 12 (retained in present text), and presents the final two lines of the present text as a single long line: present text follows a backslash in typed emendations, indicating a line break.

Once I Did This

[629 tw]
Previously unpublished.

Sh *Everyboy*

[O'Shea tw] (819 tw; 822 tw; 825 tw)
Children of Albion (1969).

Present text follows *Children of Albion*, identical to O'Shea other than trivial difference in tab spacing. 819 abandons the typescript after the title, 822 after 12 lines. 825 includes the final six lines, differently ordered, among a further 17 lines, as follows:

Why narcosis when I am so high?
So think I am thick & thin
I am block-headed

I am being filtered by choice
No-Lovers
No-Bombs
No-Air Only as

Dying at Will
I've counted my days
I am bored with living
I've tasted the sweet juice man-made
Loved everywomen from Eve to here
Felt Adam's heart
& lost a child or two?
I remember rocking myself to sleep
in smoke dens of Soho
Thinking I was loved
But all dreams break down into dots
I no-longer care
I've kicked the world
in its own circle
& laughed at the Dead
Why?

Smoked

[O'Shea tw]
Prism 12 (1966); *Children of Albion* (1969).
Present text follows *Children of Albion*. O'Shea version has cancelled title 'Two Cauldrons'; cancelled dedication 'J.H. Lindsay', with 'SMOKED' inserted; a typewritten line redacted by hand after 'feels like lead' reads 'and one couldn't wish a greater wish'.

answer don't move

Children of Albion.
No known manuscript. Text follows *Children of Albion*, but alters 'Your' to 'You're' throughout.

Eleemosynary

[O'Shea tw]
Children of Albion.
O'Shea includes a circled date, rare among Hyatt's work, reading '(15-5-67)' – Lucy O'Shea's birthday. O'Shea version has a handwritten emendation in line commencing, 'she comes forth', inserting 'FACTS' over 'injections': present text follows *Children of Albion* in printing 'injections', but follows O'Shea at l.18, reading 'the unmasked / documents', where *Children of Albion* reads 'with unmasked / documents'; present text follows O'Shea in printing 'Babylonian' where *Children of Albion* reads 'Babyloinian'.

All Sunday Long

[O'Shea tw] (576 tw; 668 tw; 877-88 tw; 911 tw; 1043 tw)
Residu 2 (Spring 1966); *Children of Albion* (1969).
Present text follows *Children of Albion*. Unusual for the substantial variations in typescripts. 576, in italic typewriter font, aligns with the version published in *Residu*. Version in folder marked 'For Lucy For Love' reads 'sparking' rather than 'sparkling' in l.3 but is otherwise near-identical. 877, however, is more substantial and includes material from the shorter 668 (possibly complete at the time of composition, or lacking a second page in the archive). The section beginning 'I move' in 878 reads:

> In pains of hell
> I move
> cold as fish
> shaking my body.
> The pains are whipping –
> my will
> as somebody combs my body
> with an electric comb.
> My eyes long to fall out.

668 reads:

> I feel one large hand
> Tearing off the skin
> Then someone's fingers
> Start squeezing
> Inside my stomach
> Trying to make me
> Have sex
>
> The pains become greater
> As my throat is being filled
> With dirt;
> Together nothing seems to matter
> There's a fellow watching me bleeding
> It's out come out
>
> I've a been in my back
> I've been shot
> And feel mud

911 and 1043 are contiguous and taken together conform to the publication in *Residu*.

Electro-Magnet Thinking

[1558 tw]
Previously unpublished.
The inventory of Prynne papers reads 'other pages round here are part of this fragmentary work', naming 1554-5 and 1558. 1558, reproduced here, reads as a complete poem with 1554 a preparatory draft. Present text prints emended title from 'Elector-Magnet Thinking' in 1558 to 'Electro-Magnet Thinking'.

Reatity

[644-45 tw] (539-40 tw; 579 tw; 646-7 tw; 798-9 tw; O'Shea tw)
Residu 2 (Spring 1966); *Curtains* 3 (1972); *A Different Mercy* (1976).
Unusually there are two quite different extant versions of 'Reatity', featuring substantial, rather than minor, variants across six manuscripts. Present text follows 644-45, which consists of 46 lines distributed across 13 stanzas. Publication

in *A Different Mercy* closely follows this arrangement, as does 798-9. Though likely an earlier draft, Hyatt circulated this version of the poem during his lifetime, as correspondence from Wendy Oliver attests. Textual preference is based on fullness: 'Reatity' is one of Hyatt's most ambitious and sustained poems, and 644-45 presents fair copy.

The version at 539-40 features 29 lines distributed across 7 stanzas. The publication in *Residu*, which editor Dan Richter remembers was arranged by Harry Fainlight, follows this rendition. *Curtains*, in turn, prints the *Residu* setting, also found in 579 in a distinct italic typewriter font, and in a typescript in the O'Shea collection. In this compact version, stanzas 1, 5, 9, 10 and 13 of the text as printed here, are excised. The poem begins 'I am, as always, in front of a mirror' (l.6 as published here) and ends 'All night / the beauty is rolling in.' Several other lines and stanzas migrate, merge, and part.

Present text incorporates the dedication to Harry Fainlight, evident in 539-40 and in *Residu*. Present text follows 798-9 in printing 'like a bird dying in the wind' at l.10, where 644-45 and *A Different Mercy* read 'like a bird that's dying in the wind.' In all versions, there is a degree of ambiguity around the stanza divisions; present text follows *A Different Mercy*. The title developed from Lucy O'Shea's mis-typing of 'Reality'.

LYONS
[O'Shea tw]
Previously unpublished.
The typescript has 'LYONS?' handwritten and underlined at the top, suggesting some concern about the title. It is signed.

Radio-Me: The Big Send Up of Everything Around Us
[O'Shea tw]
Previously unpublished.
Handwritten subtitle with 'Radio-Me' typed above. A handwritten note reads, 'Lucy I don't ever want to see this poem again. Please take it; it's very bad'. Holograph emendation cancels 'make' in 'I make love to a dog', and alters 'forgive' in line following to 'forget'. Present text inserts lines 3-4 in stanza 6, which appear at the foot of the page with handwritten direction of their current placement. Present text inserts 'with' in 'sleep with women'. The foot of the page also includes a repeat of the first line and-a-half, deleted by hand: 'If You ever find out I am in Love with You / & You see me;'.

"re-reflections season weaker"
[648 tw]
Previously unpublished.
648 is a page of foolscap folded in half vertically. 're-reflections' runs down the left-hand side. Four other poems or poem-fragments run down the right-hand side of the sheet. The sheet has been rotated 180 degrees, with a further two typed fragments running 'up' the page.

Love Limits History
[648 tw]
Previously unpublished.
648 has the line 'love limits history' offset above the poem. This is taken as the title in the Prynne inventory, adopted in the present text.

Bored
[840 tw]
Previously unpublished.
In 840 l.15, '–bites hard work', is cancelled by hand.

My Auto-Biograth Hours
[850-53 tw]
Previously unpublished. Present text alters the title to 'My Auto-Biograph Hours'. The numbered sections may simply correspond to the 4 pages of the manuscript I can't see any previous publications?

"The world is at war"
[817 tw]
Previously unpublished.

From my father to me
[704 tw] (O'Shea tw)
Previously unpublished.
Version in O'Shea Papers gives variant line break at l.2: 'a fighting urge to kill / time.' l.5 has 'a ball' rather than 'in a ball'. O'Shea differs in capitalisation, giving full stop after 'lesson of life', 'mark of time' and 'expected me to smile.'

To my mother, dead
[712 tw] (O'Shea tw)
Previously unpublished.
In the O'Shea version the second stanza is tabbed significantly right.; it lacks 'appointment' in l.2; l.4 reads 'because no together can live'. Present text follows O'Shea in inserting a line break in 'For men are beautiful and bitter / as the earth' in l.14.

POEM ON MY BIRTH
[745 tw] (1494 tw; O'Shea tw)
A Different Mercy (1976).
Present text follows *A Different Mercy*, but retains a variant reading at l.13, 'little bull', as found in 745 and 1494; *A Different Mercy* and O'Shea both print 'little boy'.

Poem 'I tried to look for a body'
[724 tw]
Saturday Morning 1 (Spring 1976).

Freedom is a waste of paper
[678 tw] (936 tw; O'Shea tw)
Figs 3 (1980).
Lineation between versions varies, with 936 suggesting a prose poem: text follows 678 and O'Shea.

Awake
[749 tw] (797 tw; 864 tw; 896 tw; O'Shea tw)
A Different Mercy (1976).
896 and one of two copies in the O'Shea collection give the dedication 'Wendy Oliver', followed in present text. Present text does not include two dashes at the end of l.5 and 15 in 749 and the O'Shea Papers. 797 is identical to 749 after incorporating handwritten emendations.

There You Go Baby
[758-59 tw] (671 tw; 672 tw; 1075 tw; O'Shea tw)
A Different Mercy (1976); *Equofinality* 2 (1984); *Not Love Alone: A Modern Gay Anthology* (1985); *Poets on Writing: 1979-1991* (1992).
Present text follows 758-9. 671 and 672 are incomplete, the second abandoned after one line of type. 671 is titled 'T Y G Baby (2)' and includes the stanza commencing 'I think of Harlequin'. 1075 is the first half of the poem and likely matching 671. 758-59 is a full version. 671/O'Shea version in folder marked 'For Lucy For Love' include minor variant punctuation notably some line end dashes (which occur in various typescripts) at l.3, 8, and 13, not followed in present text. The publication of 'There You Go Baby' in *Not Love Alone* ends at "tails on fire", omitting the second stanza.

I am frozen with knowledge
[1017 tw] (981 tw; O'Shea tw)
A Different Mercy (1976).

There are two versions in the O'Shea papers: one capitalizes 'Time' in l.4; does not include the line '& governments dry out our thoughts'; handwritten emendation changes 'longhair on' to 'longhair of' in l.16; l.26 is in typewritten parentheses; l.28 reads '& there's bad-weather'. The same version is also followed by 'In this slaughter-house', and comparison of line-lengths and subject matter suggests that these may be one poem: accordingly, the present text prints them consecutively. 981 is unrecognizable, except for its title, and reads:

I see through words
& know my lover wears the night.

The paper crowns of my world
kick my spirit
& patch secrets over pain
but sounds laugh in me
as eyes eat my body,

Planes look for a life to kill
& men buy my death.

I am the shape of self;
see me & know pain
but I am black with wishes
& my virgin life has no pain.

Nothing holds the last trick

'In this slaughter-house'
[925 tw] (926 tw; O'Shea tw)
A Different Mercy (1976).
925 and the O'Shea version are identical, fair copy. 926 has as a single handwritten emendation, correcting the typing of 'Established'. Also see note to 'I am frozen with knowledge.'

'the earth moves on cracked mirrors'
[994 tw]
Previously unpublished.

He is a Rose
[1001 tw] (1535 tw; O'Shea tw)

A Different Mercy (1976).
The version in the O'Shea Papers does not include 'two' in l.1, and reads 'we have not woken to each-other burns' at l.11.

Age
[702 tw] (1143 tw)
Somethings (c. 1967); *A Different Mercy* (1976).
Dedication and date are only present in 1143, reading: 'FOR CRESSIDA LOVE MARK 17-10-64' with a signature. The question mark at 'Life?' is only present in 702, as a handwritten emendation.

To A Romantic (Robin)
[686 tw] (700 tw; 1157 hg; 1474 tw; O'Shea tw)
Previously unpublished.
Present text follows fair copy of 686 and O'Shea. 700 and 1474 capitalize line openings. 1157 varies in lineation, breaking most likely at the edge of the page; an emendation to 'allowed' gives 'PERMITTED'; concludes, 'The germ / of time among the stars. Lost, / Lost is this day, As winter Turns / His Fur to ice'.

OUR FRIENDSHIP BEGAN ON THE FOUNDATIONS OF BUILDING A BASEMENT.
[O'Shea tw]
Previously unpublished.

"Alas, I have corrupted beauty"
[1390 tw]
A Different Mercy (1976).
A Different Mercy follows 1390 but refers in the contents page to 'Alas, I have infected beauty'. Both *A Different Mercy* and 1390 read 'I raise to the morning' at l.2, altered in present text to 'I rise'.

THE BAYSWATER BOY
[1416 tw]
Previously unpublished.
1416 gives 'THE BAYSWATER BOY' in capitals with '(your looking queer, today)' handwritten, lowercase. l.6 reads 'love or dearth'.

THE WASTE
[728 tw] (1464 tw)
A Different Mercy (1976).
1464 draft is incomplete, but present text follows it in l.2, giving 'winds' rather than 'wind'. 1464 includes two lines emended by hand from 'But the single [unclear] of thought, wisdom / Took it's [unclear]', to read 'But thought took its course / And turned into wisdom'. Crossed out after 'clear sight' are the lines: 'And my judas lies awake / In the gutter of this body, you once loved'.

the end of this day
[1475 tw]
A Different Mercy (1976).
1475 has the title in lowercase, with typescript 'Day's End' cancelled, the present title added in hand; several alterations by hand include three hand-cancelled lines following l.16:

I look in a book for a dead poet's words
and the words are too dead to move my
                                own thoughts
by reading I am nursing the poet's pain

Poem is signed in type Mark Hyatt, with the word 'MARSHMALLOW' handwritten beneath.

THE BOY
[1482 tw]
A Different Mercy (1976).
1482 has both 'THE BOY' and 'SAVAGE' written in hand as titles.

After last night she said
[690 tw] (1510 tw; O'Shea tw)
Previously unpublished.
1510 lacks capitalization and punctuation excepting a terminal period.

Looking Back
[719tw] (1511 tw; O'Shea tw)
New Departures 7/8 and 10/11 [Double Issue] (1975); *A Different Mercy* (1976).
Present text follows 719, *A Different Mercy* and *New Departures*. 1511, an earlier draft, offers variants at l.3, reading: 'we are but surf in a storm / and it's the shadows that make' and reads 'spinning look' rather than 'glancing look' at l.9. An additional line after 'but rumbles on in darkness' reads:

for that little something
under a leaf of a tree.
The cherry flash of birth we held
gave us choice

The version with handwritten corrections also reads after 'resist':

Because we need the chance to touch flesh
and to move blood
we love, We love
to embrace the present whilst
covering the past with our hands.

Hyatt signs the poem with a pseudonym, Titian Nureyev.

Dream Of You
[1603 hg] (684 tw; 891 tw)
Previously unpublished.
684 misses the second stanza, and breaks l.10: 'burnt a smile across your / face'. 891 is titled 'Dream of You (1) & (2)'. Present text follows punctuation of 891.

Love and Hate
The Aylesford Review, IV.5 (Winter 1961-2).
No known manuscript version.

BIBLIOGRAPHY

Note: Where no title is given in a publication, the first line has been placed in quotation marks. For work titled 'Poem', the first line has been supplied in parentheses.

NOVEL

Love, Leda, edited by Luke Roberts (London: Peninsula Press, 2023).

CHAPBOOKS

How Odd (Eltham: Blacksuede Boot Press & Ferry Press, 1973). 150 copies.

Blacksuede Boot Press was edited by Barry MacSweeney and Elaine Randell; Ferry Press by Andrew Crozier. Cover by Paul McSweeney. Contents:

Taken; Soul Saver; Border Line; Paddy of Lancashire; Poor Sod; Fool; It Never Sleeps; Messing About; A Village Lad; Puffed-out; Home; Poem ['Trying to remember what memory']; A Definite Choice; Work and Wonder; Tiger in the Mind; How Odd.

Eleven Poems (London: Ted Cavanagh, 1974). 200 copies.
'Hand-set & printed by Ted Cavanagh.'
Contents:
1 POEMS ABOUT POETRY: i. Dice; ii. Bootless; iii. Mug's Game; iv. 'Rattling focus...'.
2 ART WORKING: The Composer's Fingers.
3 INNER SPACE: i. Daggers; ii. Schizoid.
4 NARRATIVE POEMS: i.

Tame; ii. A Regular Guy.
5 PASTORAL POEMS: i. Wine; ii. Inconclusive Engagement.

A Different Mercy (Cambridge: Infernal Methods, 1976). 250 copies.
Infernal Methods was edited by Nigel Wheale and David Trotter.

'This selection of poems by Mark Hyatt (1940-1972) was edited from photocopies of manuscripts left after his death. Apart from a very few silent corrections of obvious errors of transcription, the original text, as we have it, of each poem has been reproduced exactly. The classification of material into four sections is our own and in no way definitive. Section I assumes the centrality of lyric intent to Hyatt's work, while sections II and III cover aspects of the 'history of self'. Section IV includes more experimental writing and in one case (pages 64-6) the passage of a poem from draft to 'final' version ['I am Frozen with Knowledge']. The manuscript of 'The End of This Day' has 'marshmallow' scribbled across it. Other work by Hyatt has appeared in magazines, and in two booklets: HOW ODD (1973) and ELEVEN POEMS (1974).'
Contents:
I. 'Alas, I have infected beauty'; Poem ['I have to feel for words']; 'Soon the mind will be heavy'; Universal Eyes; 'the jade thieves carve the wind'; 'white angels move in the wind'; 'I have drunken the bromide'; Honey Child; Composing; 'just woke up to a lot of light'; Poem ['I tried to look for a body'];

Age; 'a high height when thinking';
'elaine is overpowering'; Awake;
Delicate; High Blues; 'I want it now
baby honey'; 'The rose is a ring of
blood'; He is a Rose.

II. 'History of self'; Poem on My
Birth; The Boy; Puberty of Puck;
'from the poor freak streets comes
a lad'; I'm Trying; 'Now I live in
the north country'; There You Go
Baby; Hope; Shropshire Service;
'In this slaughter-house'; The
Waste; Is it Now; Looking Back; So
So; Deep Silence.

III. Country Poem; 'It's deep
inside, this nothingness'; Climb;
The End of this Day; 'The eternal
day breaks out'; 'The moth is back,
just peeled out of the skin'; Green
Life; Look What They Do; A Shiner;
'Smoke flowing out of the hill'; 'love
in the shadow of summer'; 'Two
queers live on a hill'.

IV. Dazzle: Lament Diagram;
Extended Movement; Reatity;
God-Golliwog; 'sleep in my eyes if
you want a home'; I am Frozen with
Knowledge.

Randel's Vision (Odense, Denmark:
Spirit Mimeo, c. 1971). c. 20 copies.
Spirit Mimeo was edited by
Peter Riley.

John Wilkinson writes: 'A pam-
phlet preceded the three listed, but
its publication status is precarious:
Randell's Vision [sic]. Peter Riley,
spirit mimeo edition, Odense
Denmark c1971. 10pp. about 20
copies. Even the publisher has
no copy. Information would be
welcome.' (Wilkinson 2010). Prose
narrative, published with variation
in *Grosseteste Review* and *Drug
Tales*, below.

ANTHOLOGIES

Children of Albion, edited by Michael
Horowitz (Harmondsworth: Pen-
guin, 1969).
Smoked; All Sunday Long; Sh
Everyboy; answer don't move;
Eleemosynary

Drug Tales, edited by Duncan Fal-
lowell (London: Hamish Hamilton,
1979)
Randel

*Not Love Alone: A Modern Gay
Anthology*, edited by Martin Hum-
phries (London: Gay Men's Press,
1985).
Nerves Blotted Out; There You
Go Baby; Individual

Poets on Writing: 1979-1991, edited
by Denise Riley (Houndmills: Mac-
millan, 1992).
'White angels move in the wind';
There You Go Baby; Extended
Movement

JOURNALS

The Aylesford Review 4.2 (Spring
1961), edited by Brocard Sewell.
All From Eden

The Aylesford Review 4.5 (Winter
1961-2), edited by Brocard Sewell.
Love and Hate

The Aylesford Review 4.8 (Autumn
1962), edited by Brocard Sewell.
Autumn Time

The Aylesford Review 5.3 (Summer
1963), edited by Brocard Sewell.
Child

Breakthru International Poetry Magazine 17 (July/August 1964), edited by Ken Geering.

Poem ['Older Generation']

Canards du siècle present (1970), edited by Anthony Barnett.

Psst!

Collection 7 (Autumn 1970), edited by Peter Riley.

This Poem; Headache; Individual; Cat Poem

Collection 7, Supplement (1970), edited by Peter Riley.

To A Woman; The Mark of Sleepy Laughter

The Curiously Strong III.5 (January 19th 1971), edited by Ian Patterson and Fred Buck.

Is It You?; Poem ['Please go and tell']

The Curiously Strong III.7 (May 19th 1971), edited by Ian Patterson and Fred Buck.

I'm Trying; I Know; You Said

The Curiously Strong: Final Issue IV.9 & 10 (1975), edited by Ian Patterson.

True Homosexual Love

Curtains 3 (1972), edited by Paul Buck.

Note: 'this issue is for: Mark Hyatt (1940–1972).' Buck provides 'towards a bibliography'.

Reatity; The Mark of Sleepy Laughter; To a Woman

Earth Ship 7 (December 1971/January 1972), edited by Kris Hemensley.

It's All in the Past Now; Pretty Common

Equofinality 2 (1984), edited by Rod Mengham and John Wilkinson.

So Much For Life; So So; There You Go Baby; Psst!; Green Life; Individual; Nerves Blotted Out; Come into the World; True Homosexual Love; A Dream

Figs 3 (c. 1980), edited by Tony Baker.

Freedom Is a Waste of Paper; 'England is my bedroom'; 'Guard the mouse that lives in a box'; Broken Life (for Peter Swan); 'I am where I dream naturally'; Something Found; 'Wearily I drag the mind'

Global Tapestry Journal - All Power to the Imagination issue 3 (February 1972) edited by Dave Cunliffe.

Yes!; In of Lonliness

Global Tapestry Journal 4 (Homage to Kenneth Patchen Issue) (February 1973), edited by Dave Cunliffe.

Note: "Mark Hyatt (1940-1972). Mark gave me the following confessional poem shortly before he died. I enjoyed reading with him at Tina Morris's Poets meet Folk open mixed-media session & at the Living Poetry Earle Birney reading. The inquest verdict was suicide from an overdose of asprin & mandrax. DC"

VD JESUS CHRIST; New Brave Wired Ones

Global Tapestry Journal 8 (September 1979), edited by Dave Cunliffe.

Note: Also includes Michael Horovitz, 'for Mark Hyatt (1940-1972).

Growing Peas; A Regular Guy; The Best of People; Inconclusive Engagement; About Elizabeth; Wine; Dice

Greedy Shark (1973), edited by Ian Patterson and Barry MacSweeney.

Hello; She's Right to Look at You; Between You and Humanity

Grosseteste Review 5.3 (Autumn 1972), edited by Tim Longville.
Randel's Vision

Grosseteste Review 7.1-3 (Summer 1974), edited by Tim Longville.
'puzzled by imagination'; 'desert bones'; Sad Day; 'The mind bounces on the road'; 'I am trying to find something'

Human Handkerchief 3 (Summer 1974), editors include Simon Pettet, Ralph Hawkins and Douglas Oliver.
'in a bedroom on a hill'; In English; 'Hark! the dearie mark'

Joe DiMaggio 2 (1972), edited by John Robinson.
'Heaven endeavours to reward', 'They say one man came back', The Queer Affair, Cornelius

Lift (c. 1970), edited by K. Keighley / Barnoldswick Congregational.
Note: 'Three Poems by guest writer Mark Hyatt':
'To the father of Christmas', 'So the story goes', 'Lo to life this morning'

Lift (c. 1970), edited by K. Keighley / Barnoldswick Congregational.
Homewalk

Lift (c. 1970), edited by K. Keighley / Barnoldswick Congregational.
Note: 'Poems from the Thoughts of Mark Hyatt':
Question My Answer; Slogan; Whitey; The Last Cry

Lift (c. 1970), edited by K. Keighley / Barnoldswick Congregational.
Note: 'Poems To Think On by

Mark Hyatt':
Jesus; Holy Hands; The Day's Sage

The Literary Supplement 2 (Friday 13 October 1972), edited by Anthony Barnett.
Village Blues

The Literary Supplement 20 (August 1974), edited by Anthony Barnett.
Nerves Blotted Out; 'between chaos I come'; Delicate; 'that's it really, nothing too big under wind'; Deep Silence; No Mercy

Musics 10 (November 1976), edited by Peter Riley.
Note: 'Hyatt died in 1972. In the manuscript the second stanza is scored through.'
The Food of Love

New Departures 7/8 and 10/11 [Double Issue] (1975), edited by Michael Horovitz.
Looking back; In Cornwall; Border Line; The Song of a Madman; Blocked; Loverman; Down and Out; Headache; Love Me Through Your Mind; The Head of the Eye; O Poem

New Departures 13: 'Lucky Dip Anthology' (1981), edited by Michael Horovitz.
To Poets Unprinted; All from Eden

Palantir 15 (July 1980), edited by Jim Burns.
Growing Peas

Pause 2 (Winter 1969/Spring 1970), edited by Deirdre Farrell.
So Much For Life

Poetry Review 65.2/3 (1975), edited by Eric Mottram.

'I see heat as a bird in the universe'; Growing Peas; Small Things; Poem ['Hunting key holes for pity']; 'the golden penis still stands'

Prism Sixty Six (1966), edited by Wes Magee.
Be of good cheer; My Son; Cinema

Prism 11 (c. 1966), edited by Wes Magee.
No extant copy located; unknown contribution by Mark Hyatt.

Prism 12 (1966), edited by Wes Magee.
Smoked

Prism 14 (April 1967), edited by Wes Magee.
Angela; 'Imagine hysterical war'

Prism 15, *A Prism Anthology* (June 1967), edited by Wes Magee.
Death; Don't Let Anybody Breathe on You

Residu 2 (Spring 1966), edited by Daniel Richter.
Reatity; All Sunday Long; The Head of the Eye

Sal Mimeo 13 (2013), edited by Larry Fagin.
Puberty of Puck

Saturday Morning 1 (Spring 1976), edited by Simon Pettet.
Note: 'the version published in *Musics* 1976 retains the second stanza but record it's been struck through; here the editor keeps the final line, but excises the rest of stanza 2'.
'down and out', 'poem: I tried to look for a body'; 'the food of love'; 'occasional poem'

Skylight 2 (Winter-Spring 1972), edited by Peter Baker.
Pickpocketpoets; Hyde Park

Somethings (c. 1967), edited by Dave Austin and Kay Anderson.
Woman; Age

Spanner 7 (March 1976), edited by Allen Fisher, though this issue credited to CRUST.
'Dear William' [Prose, letter dated 5.2.72]

Strange Faeces 8 Special Abolition of Slavery Issue (1972), edited by Allen Fisher.
SADDAY; The Best of People; The Vista

Turpin 7/8 (February 1974), edited by Jeremy Helm, Jeremy Harding, Maurice Slawinski, and Martin Thom.
'the jade thieves carve the wind'; 'i'm camping'; Of Something Else; 'Read the Book of Centuries'

CRITICISM

Michael Horovitz, 'Foreword', *New Departures* Double Issue 7/8, 10/11 (1975).

Rob Jackaman, *The Course of English Surrealist Poetry Since the 1930s* (Lewiston, NY: Edwin Mellen, 1989).

Robert Sheppard, *The Poetry of Saying: British Poetry and Its Discontents, 1950-2000* (Liverpool University Press, 2005).

Geoffrey Thurley, *The Ironic Harvest: English Poetry in the Twentieth Century* (New York: St Martin's Press, 1974).

John Wilkinson, 'Mark Hyatt's
Poésie Brute.' *Hidden Agendas:
Unreported Poetics,* edited by Louis
Armand (Prague: Litteraria Pragen-
sia, 2010).

John Wilkinson, *Lyric in Its Times:
Temporalities in Verse, Breath, and Stone*
(London: Bloomsbury, 2019).

John Wilkinson, 'Mark Hyatt: A
Different Mercy.' *Perfect Bound* 3
(Cambridge, 1977).

ACKNOWLEDGEMENTS

We are conscious that this is only the most recent attempt to publish a collection of Mark Hyatt's poems. Our profound and foremost thanks go to Dylan Hyatt, executor of his father's estate, both for permission to publish this material and for the patience he has shown during the long gestation of the collection.

We are grateful to Hyatt's friends, Lucy and Mick O'Shea, who gave us fresh impetus as the project neared completion. We thank Jill Catlow, Wendy Prahms (formerly Wendy Oliver), and the late Laura Del-Rivo for sharing their memories. Peter Baker was an exceptionally generous correspondent. Dave Cunliffe, who sadly passed away during the editing of this book, was also unstinting in his support for Hyatt's work.

Without J.H. Prynne, the present book would have been impossible to put together. He held Hyatt's papers safely for more than four decades in Gonville & Caius, Cambridge, now transferred to his archive in the Cambridge University Library. We are grateful for his willingness, and that of the estate, to release the material temporarily so that a copy could be made for our consultation. He answered our questions with customary patience, exactitude, and encouragement.

Peter Riley made a partial transcription of Hyatt's archive in the 1970s and gathered many of the extant publications which became the source for various posthumous publications; Peter generously supplied us with his collection of material to begin our own editorial work.

Neil Pattison's investigations led to conversations with Riley, Ian Patterson, and other poets, which set the ball rolling for this edition more than a dozen years ago. Special thanks to John Wilkinson, who has engaged critically with Hyatt's work since the mid-1970s, and who has been key to keeping Hyatt's name in circulation.

Many other editors, publishers, booksellers, friends, and friends-of-friends kindly responded to our requests for information, including: Paul Buck, Jean Crozier, David Elliott of Quartet Books, Duncan Fallowell, Gillian Figures, Michael Haslam, Ralph Hawkins, Wes Magee, Rod Mengham, Drew Milne, Tina Morris, Wendy Mulford, Opal L. Nations, Brian Patten, Vincent Quinn, Elaine Randell, Dan Richter, Denise Riley, James Riley, Will Shutes, Keston Sutherland, Barry Tebb, Martin Thom, David Trotter, and Nigel Wheale. Bruce Wilkinson was indefatigable in tracking some of the connections local to Blackburn, and a generous correspondent.

Thanks to James Cummins, Kerstin Fest, Sarah Hayden, and Rachel Warriner for accepting a paper on Hyatt's work at the University College Cork conference '*Étant donnés*' (2013). Our gratitude to Matt ffytche (University of Essex) and John Wilkinson (University of Chicago) for accepting a short discussion piece as part of their Outsider Writing Project in 2017.

Our thanks to John Wells of the Cambridge University Library, alumni archivists at Cambridge, and archivists and librarians at the British Library, University of Nottingham Library, University of Sheffield's Western Bank Library, Newcastle University's Philip Robinson Library, University of Indiana's Lilly Library, and University College London's Special Collections Library.

This edition began with Miles Champion as co-editor who, due to his generosity in supporting and editing the work of other poets, had to take a step back. Sam wishes to thank Luke for joining this project with the vast enthusiasm necessary to turn something daunting into a pleasure.

In addition to those named above, gratitude is due for information, correspondence, and encouragement to: Sara Crangle, Tom Crompton, David Grundy, Dom Hale, Rob Halpern, Edward Holberton, Mark Johnson, Tom Jones, Michael Kindellan, Peter Larkin, Adam Piette, Robin Purves, the late Tom Raworth, Eleanor Roberts, Mark Roberts, Peter Target, and Amy Tobin. Thanks to Stephen Motika, Rissa Hochberger, Gia Gonzales, Lindsey Boldt and the wonderful team at Nightboat Books for sharing our excitement in the project, and for their acumen in presenting this work to the reader.

Finally, we want to acknowledge Hyatt's partners for their role in nurturing and preserving Hyatt's writing, in particular Donald 'Atom' Haworth, who we were unable to trace despite following dozens of lines of inquiry, and Cressida Lindsay, who passed away in 2010.

MARK HYATT (1940-1972) lived at the center and the fringes of the bohemian underground in 1960s Britain. In the half-century since his death, his work has been known almost exclusively by word-of-mouth. Drawing on a full range of archival sources, *So Much For Life* is the first comprehensive edition of his poems.

SAM LADKIN works at the University of Sussex, and writes about poetry in relation to other artforms.

LUKE ROBERTS is a poet and writer. He works at King's College London.

NIGHTBOAT BOOKS

Nightboat Books, a nonprofit organization, seeks to develop audiences for writers whose work resists convention and transcends boundaries. We publish books rich with poignancy, intelligence, and risk. Please visit nightboat.org to learn about our titles and how you can support our future publications.

The following individuals have supported the publication of this book. We thank them for their generosity and commitment to the mission of Nightboat Books:

Kazim Ali
Anonymous (4)
Aviva Avnisan
Jean C. Ballantyne
The Robert C. Brooks Revocable Trust
Amanda Greenberger
Rachel Lithgow
Anne Marie Macari
Elizabeth Madans
Elizabeth Motika
Thomas Shardlow
Benjamin Taylor
Jerrie Whitfield & Richard Motika

This book is made possible, in part, by grants from the New York City Department of Cultural Affairs in partnership with the City Council and the New York State Council on the Arts Literature Program.